I Was a Slave

PLIGHT OF A KING

Race Cummings

Legacy Publishing

Atlanta, Georgia

Cummings, Race.
 I Was a Slave: Plight of a King/Race Cummings. —1st ed.

Publisher: Amazon Digital Services LLC

ISBN-13: 978-1530995936

ISBN-10: 1530995930

Contents

Dedication

This book is dedicated first to Yahweh, for being there and understanding a Black man when no one else seemed to understand; to my Legacy Crew; and to all those people who have been with me from the beginning and understand the Black experience.

"Change will not come if we wait for some other person
or some other time. We are the ones we've been waiting for.
We are the change that we seek."

- President Barack Obama

Introduction

W hen we think of the word "king" we think of someone born into royalty; someone born into power and privilege. A king is a leader—first of *himself,* and then a leader of others. A king oversees his kingdom; he knows the people inside his kingdom, and if he doesn't, he makes it his business to find out who they are, what their needs are, and how their talents can enhance the kingdom. A king makes decisions; he makes decrees for the good of the kingdom.

A king calls the shots. He is reverenced and honored, and in many cases, envied and feared. But even more importantly, a true king, a benevolent king, a just king, is loved by his people.

If you are African American, you have probably heard a relative, friend or even an enemy boasting that your people (our people) come from kings. When you heard it, it may have sounded strange to your ears. It may have even made you smile. But the thing is, it's true. African Americans come from a royal lineage.

There was Affonso I (1506-1540), the visionary; Hannibal, ruler of Carthage (247-183 BC); Mansa Kankan Musa, King of Mali (1306-1332) who was reportedly worth $400 billion in today's currency; the dazzlingly beautiful Cleopatra VII, Queen of Egypt (69 – 30 BC)[1] of whom many books have been written and movies have been produced; and the famous and quite elusive Makeda, Queen of Sheba (960 BC), the wise woman who reportedly "made the long and difficult journey to Jerusalem"[2] to learn from the wisdom of the great King Solomon."

This is a shortlist of only a few of our ancestors of royal blood, but it is still quite impressive. A king (or queen) is groomed for greatness, rules with wisdom and equity, and leaves a legacy. And as the descendants of kings and queens, should we do any less? Of course not. We should do the same—especially where our men are concerned.

But do we?

This and other questions fuel the framework of this book: namely, how many African Americans are aware of their royal lineage, what are they doing about that knowledge, and how can their actions help to uplift our African American communities?

[1] Before We Were Slaves: Great Kings and Queens of Africa, by Ashley Snowden. https://thesummary.wordpress.com/2011/08/28/before-we-were-slaves-great-kings-and-queens-of-africa/. Retrieved January 7, 2016.
[2] 10 African Kings and Queens Whose Stories Must Be told on Film by AtlantaBlackStar.com staff. http://atlantablackstar.com/2013/12/07/10-african-kings-and-queens-whose-stories-must-be-told-on-film/. Retrieved on January 7, 2016.

CHAPTER 1

Who Are We?

N o matter who tries to argue otherwise, African Americans are descended from kings and queens. But is the mere knowledge of this fact enough, or do we need more than just this faded label to understand who we really are?

The answer is YES, we need more. The average African American has no clue who they really are because to begin with, they don't know who we *were*. They don't know their own history. African Americans have lost their identity. And in case you're wondering, this didn't just happen in the last generation. It happened many, many years ago.

We all know the story: African Americans came here as slaves, were forbidden to eat their own foods, wear their own types of clothing and speak their own languages. They were forced to learn a new culture—fast; they were tossed into the proverbial twelve feet of water and warned to either "sink or swim."

They (we) swam. We know this because we—their descendants, are still here. But to stay afloat they had to lose something; shed some weight that might possibly drag them down underwater. That "weight", unfortunately, was memory and tradition. African Americans had to forget the old ways, change the way things were done, learn to adapt in a harsh new environment. It was the only way to survive.

They had to forget, and that's exactly what they did.

Today, African Americans are the only group of people who aren't really a "group" of people; they (we) are actually a bunch of individuals who have been lumped into a group because of the color of their skin. But large group or not, the truth is that African Americans are alone. They are not liked by anyone, not even themselves, and they cannot trust anyone, most especially not their own people.

Not so long ago, a Black man was once everyone's pick-me-up. What is a pick-me-up? It's like a scapegoat. It means that at one time, no matter how poorly a person, family or group was doing in life, no matter what race they happened to be or what rung of the socioeconomic ladder they were on, as long as they were not African American, they felt that they were doing just fine.

Why? Because other races—Caucasians, East Indians and even true Africans—believed that they were better than us. Somewhere along the path of your life, you may have heard one or more of them say, "Well, at least I'm not an African American." Which is to say that no matter how bad things may be for them, they haven't hit bottom because at least they are not African American.

That was then. Now, however, our country has an African American president who has not only served one term, he is finishing up his second! We have African American millionaires and African Americans professionals appointed to power positions in the country. Our African American women are also making great strides, both professionally and financially. For example, Michelle Obama is the first African American First Lady of the United States of America (2008-2016). Condoleeza Rice served as the 66th United States

Secretary of State (2005-2009) under President George W. Bush. And Dr. Carla D. Hayden was only recently tapped by President Barack Obama to serve as the 14th Librarian of Congress.

For these and other reasons, the same people who once comforted themselves by chanting "At least I'm not African American" cannot use this as a pick-me-up anymore. They have had a rude awakening. They have discovered that they cannot outperform us or out-think us or out-earn us as they were once assured that they could, and now they don't know how to react. Those same people who once had the "at least I'm not African American" mindset simply cannot use this mindset anymore.

That being said, the Black man born into the African American culture still has problems with everyone; he has problems with society, the law, the corporate system, and even with his women. This in itself is a real tragedy, especially since African Americans ruled the world first, colonized the world first, and were already settled in certain parts of the world—including America—long before the white man ever stepped foot on the shoreline.

The oldest map of the world is from Africa, and Africans are responsible for some of the most famous art and other items. And yet, despite all this, America does not acknowledge our African American culture and neither do African Americans. Being born African American usually leads to the belief that "white is right." This is largely due to the fact that African American history has been transfigured, misconstrued and manipulated to make Caucasian history seem more glorious and more progressive. Caucasians have indeed created some things, but they have also taken credit for many concepts, inventions and procedures that are purely African American in origin.

And that brings us back to the fact that nobody likes African Americans. Other races emulate African American dances, tan their skin to look "exotic" like African Americans, dance our dances, mimic our handshakes, plump up their lips so that they are full like ours, braid their hair, use African American vernacular, ogle our women, and envy our strength, stamina and ingenuity. But they don't want anyone to compare them to African Americans. They don't like African Americans.

Unfortunately, African Americans don't like African Americans either. Did you know that in African American culture, the white man is not the Black man's competition? That's right, in many cases white men have no reason to compete with Black men because they already hold a position of power. The Black man's competition in most cases is another Black man—or a Black woman.

It's sad but true. And one other thing you may want to make note of: If you want to know who's going to kill you, it probably won't be the white man or the Oriental man or the East Indian man. It most likely will be an African American male. Why? Because African Americans have been groomed since slavery to be violent toward each other in more ways than they have ever been toward other races. In many ways, we are our own worst enemies.

CHAPTER 2

The Black Man's America

"We hold these truths to be self-evident, that all men are created equal,
that they are endowed by their Creator with certain unalienable Rights,
that among these are Life, Liberty and the pursuit of Happiness."
—From The Declaration of Independence

A merica is the land of the free and the brave; the land where you can freely pursue life, liberty, happiness—and capitalism, too, if you have a mind to.

According to Thomas Jefferson, "Nothing can stop the man with the right mental attitude from achieving his goal [and] nothing on earth can help the man with the wrong mental attitude." Abraham Lincoln said that "You can have anything you want—if you want it badly enough. You can be anything you want to be, do anything you set out to accomplish, if you hold to that desire with singleness of purpose." And George Washington said, "Ninety-nine percent of the failures come from people who have the habit of making excuses."

These are a few quotes from America's founding fathers as they worked to capture the definition of the American Dream and put it down on paper. But did these words include everyone back then? Do they include everyone now? Do these ideas represent the Black man's America? America was not and is not supposed to be a place of persecution or racism or killing or enslavement; it was founded on the idea of freedom and happiness. But is there freedom and happiness for all?

African American men (and women) have been trying to be free and happy in American society since the idea of America was born. The word "idea" is used here because that is what America is. It's not simply a land or a place, it's a way of life; a way of thinking. This continent was already here before Columbus actually set foot on its shore, so that is why I refer to it as an idea and not necessarily a country.

Researcher and writer Runoko Rashidi (Atlanta Black Star) writes that the Olmec, an early people of Meso-America, settled the Mexican Gulf Coast and have been labeled as the first civilization of the western hemisphere, as they surpassed their neighbors in an attempt to settle certain problems of living together (government, defense, religion, family, property, science and art), and laid the foundation of American civilization."[3]

The sculptural and skeletal remains found of ancient Olmec sites in the pre-Columbus "new world" provide the most conclusive evidence yet discovered concerning the presence of African people in America before Columbus."[4] Also, according to Dr. David Imhotep, "Egyptian artifacts found across North America from the Algonquin writings on the East Coast to the artifacts and Egyptian place names in the Grand Canyon" are all signs of an early arrival in the Americas by Africans.[5]

----

[3] Rashidi, Rumoko. Before Enslavement: Africa's Ancient Diaspora. *Atlanta Black Star.* AtlantaBlackStar.com. http://atlantablackstar.com/2014/09/14/enslavment-africas-ancient-diaspora/ Retrieved on January 8, 2016.

[4] Ibid.

[5] Imhotep, Dr. David. The First Americans were Africans: Documented Evidence.

This confirms that blacks were in this country long before Columbus, and yet today's African American is still trying to "make it" in American society.   That is because African Americans have historically been oppressed in America. According to *Five Faces of Oppression* by Iris Young, oppression is "the exercise of tyranny by a ruling group and it comes in five stages: violence, exploitation, marginalization, powerlessness, and cultural imperialism."[6]

Here are Ms. Young's definitions:

1. **Violence:** any behavior involving physical force intended to hurt, damage, or kill someone or something.

2. **Exploitation:** the act of using people's labors to produce profit while not compensating them fairly.

3. **Marginalization:** relegating or confining a group of people to a lower social standing or outer limit or edge of society.

4. **Powerlessness:** to not have the status or authority to do or achieve certain things. To not be allowed to develop capacities or make decisions; to be exposed to disrespectful treatment because of lowered status; to fall into a "culture of silence" and become so powerless that they do not even talk about their oppression; to produce a culture wherein it is forbidden to even mention the injustices that are being committed.

5. **Cultural Imperialism:** taking the culture of the ruling class and establishing it as the norm.

Do you recognize any of these "faces of oppression?" Have you experienced any of them? All of them? Have African Americans as a people and a community experienced any or all of them? The answer to this latter question would be most decidedly YES. In fact, Ms.

---

[6] Young, Iris. Five Faces of Oppression. "Oppression, Privilege and Resistance." McGraw Hill, Boston. 2004.

Young's definitions are all so obvious that examples are not even needed.

In the meantime, the Black man has been victimized by individuals and groups alike, throughout his American residency. Many times the American government also participated in this victimization. In a book called *Medical Apartheid: The Dark History of Medical Experimentation on Black Americans from Colonial Times to the Present,* African American author Harriet Washington explains how Blacks were experimented on during slavery and were little more than human sacrifices in the name of finding cures for certain sicknesses like typhoid or sunstroke.

Some candid examples include: "A black man who was injected with plutonium in 1945 to see what effect it had on the human body; the CIA and the US military in the early 1950s released close to half a million mosquitoes infected with yellow fever and dengue fever into several black neighborhoods in Florida to see if they could be used as an effective weapon of war; African American prisoners were used as guinea pigs to test toothpaste, skin cream, hair dye, and soap for pharmaceutical companies, and to test radioactive, toxic, and mind-altering drugs for the US military; and 600 Tuskegee airmen were subjected to a secret government study of the effects of syphilis on the human body."[7]

There were many more experiments than these, but these certainly do show that the government has thought nothing about destroying the Black man—and in many cases, made it a point to do so from the very beginning. And as for African American advancement since those early times, "Black people remain crowded into the lowest rungs of the ladder... [and] many of the basic industries that once

─────────────────

[7] How the US Government Used Black People as Guinea Pigs. New African Magazine. NewAfricanMagazine.com. http://newafricanmagazine.com/medical-scandal/. Retrieved on January 8, 2016.

employed Black people have closed down; employers are more likely to *hire* a white person with a criminal record than a Black person without one, and [employers] are 50% more likely to follow up on a resume with a "white-sounding" name than an identical resume with a "Black-sounding" name."[8]

In housing, Black people "face the highest levels of racial residential segregation in the world—shunted into neglected neighborhoods lacking decent parks and grocery stores and often with no hospitals at all."[9] "Black infants face [medical] mortality rates comparable to those in third world countries"[10] and today's schools "are more segregated than they have been since the 1960s."[11] They also have fewer resources than their white counterparts and are set up to fail.

The statistics go on. They also beg the question, why is this the reality of the Black man's America? What, exactly, are white people so afraid of when it comes to the Black man?

Perceptions: How the World Sees Us

What does the white man see when he looks at a Black man? Better yet, what does *anyone* see? People—including the Black man— see little more than a whirlwind. They see a hot mess. They see an accident looking for a place to happen. They also see the propaganda of the "Black Lives Matter" movement that is little more than a

---

[8] Pager, Devah. "The Mark of a Criminal Record," *American Journal of Sociology*, Volume 108, Number 5, March 2003, pp. 937-75. http://www.nber.org/papers/w9873.pdf

[9] Massey, Douglas. *Categorically Unequal: The American Stratification System*, Russell Sage Foundation, New York, 2007.
[http://www.faireconomy.org/files/StateOfDream_01_16_08_Web.pdf

[10] Smiley, Tavis, editor. *The Covenant with Black America*, Third World Press, Chicago, 2006, as cited from David Satcher's essay at the book's website covenantwithblackamerica.com.
[http://www.covenantwithblackamerica.com/covenant/health_wellbeing/]

[11] Orfield, Gary and Chungmei Lee, "Historic Reversals, Accelerating Resegregation, and the Need for New Integration Strategies," Civil Rights Project, UCLA, August 2007. http://www.civilrights.org/assets/pdfs/aug-2007-desegregation-report.pdf

facade, because the truth is, if the Black man was truly as concerned about his community as he claims through the Black Lives Matter campaign, the community would not be in the situation it is in today. There would not be rampant drugs and Black-on-Black crime, absentee fathers, out-of-control gangs, and too many single mothers to count.

When people look at the Black community, they see leaders who prostitute Civil Rights; leaders who call themselves Civil Rights leaders because they see dollar signs in the label, and not because they think they can help anyone. They also see a complete lack of accountability. They hear about Black-on-Black crime on a daily basis, drive-by shootings, drug deals and gang initiations, and made-for-TV movies about Black children practically raising themselves because their parents are on hard drugs.

They see a community, a people without accountability; a people who conveniently blame others for their present condition. They see people who claim they want a better life but are not doing anything to bring a better life about. In other words, if the Black community's agenda truly is to build and enhance and sustain the culture, the solution must be that African Americans will take accountability for their own decisions and their own community.

Fantasizing about "killing the white people" or overturning the government are just that; fantasies. They are not going to happen, period. Nothing will change African American communities or make them better except that the African Americans in those communities must be the ones to affect the change. African Americans *must* take accountability for their actions. They must be willing to do something more than just talk about the problems and complain. Until they do, things will only get worse. And yes, when and if it these things do happen, it's true that they won't wipe out every problem in our community. We will still have issues, but at least we won't have as many as we had. They will be at a minimum.

Internalized Racism

We have explored the many ways that white people and the world in general sees us. But there is another perspective we must explore if we are going to solve some of the problems in the African American community. We must explore how we as African Americans see ourselves.

Just what do we see when we look in the mirror? What do we see when we're in a crowded room full of non-white persons and we spy another African American mingling among the masses? Do we see someone we can converse with, talk to, and compare the similarities in our journey to where we are now? Or do we see someone we feel we must avoid pairing off with at all costs because they are "Black like us" and others might accuse us of gravitating toward them in an effort to be different, whisper secrets, or to be stand-offish?

In an About.com article by Nadra Kareem Nittle called *"What is Internal Racism,"* Nittle defines it this way: "In a society where racial prejudice thrives in politics, communities, institutions and popular culture, it's difficult for racial minorities to avoid absorbing the racist messages that constantly bombard them. Thus, even people of color sometimes adopt a white supremacist mindset that results in self-hatred and hatred of their respective racial group."[12]

As a result of this internalized racism, African Americans may actually hate other African Americans and strive to separate themselves from them. They may discriminate against another African American whom they consider to be too dark or too light; whose nose

---

[12] Nittle, Nadra Kareem. "What is Internal Racism?" About News. About.com. http://racerelations.about.com/od/understandingrac1/a/internalizedracism.htm. Retrieved January 11, 2016.

is too big or wide or whose hair is not worn in a manner they feel is acceptable to represent African Americans.

It is important to note, however, that those who suffer from internal racism don't just abhor other African Americans; they also abhor themselves. They may hate their own looks, mannerisms, speech, neighborhood, family members, and traditions, and they may long to portray a completely different picture so that they are "accepted" by white society.

Consider the case of Shelly Williams, a Black woman who appeared on The Judge Mathis Show in 2009 and claimed that "90% of all Black women are evil, backstabbing and hateful." Ms. Williams also made the rounds on other shows like the Wendy Williams Show and the Judge Alex Show, and stated that she "doesn't even like to admit that she's Black, and is in the process of changing her appearance." When Judge Mathis asked her race, she said, "I don't say I'm Black, I just say I'm human." Judge Mathis then told her that she *is* Black and she repeatedly answered, "No, I'm not!" She went on to say that she refuses to be friends with Black people.

This internal hatred has been known to lead to skin bleaching, hair weaves, wearing "blue" or "green" contact lenses, "talking white" and a myriad of other responses. Judge Mathis' response to this woman was: "You just hate yourself. And that's where a lot of the crime—Blacks killing each other, Black-on-Black crime, fratricide (the killing of one's brother or sister)—comes from. Sociologists theorize it's because of self-hate. Because if you don't like yourself, and don't think much of yourself, you're certainly not going to think much of your brother...or someone within your race."[13]

Let me stop for a moment and point something: I don't mean to insinuate that every person of color who wears a weave or changes

---

[13] The Judge Mathis Show. "Ashamed of Her Race." Season Ten: 2008-2009. 11/12/2008

their eye color hates the fact that they are Black. On the contrary, many African American women relax or straighten their hair because it is more manageable than wearing it natural. Also, many women and men use skin bleachers to even out the tone of their splotchy skin. The woman I just described from the Judge Mathis Show was the extreme.

The pressures of belonging to a society where white racist messages pelt a Black person's ears day and night, and where books, television, publishing companies and movies are largely "whitewashed" are strong influences on internalized racism. But these are not the only factors. African Americans make war, however invisible, on themselves, too. Many darker-skinned African Americans are laughed at, ostracized and otherwise rejected by their own African American society. Dark- and light-skinned African Americans who are not considered to act "as Black as they should" are often called "Oreo," "Uncle Tom" or "Bougie" (aspiring to a higher class than one belongs to) by other Blacks.

Dark-skinned African Americans are called all sorts of names by both Blacks and whites, including "darkie," "midnight," "silver bells" and "coon." During one of comedian Katt Williams' stand-up routines, he mentioned appearing on the *Flavor Flav Comedy Central Roast*, during which Flav would be called "A big, black, sizzle-y, crisped-y, crackle-y, crunched-y coon." Although this line received many laughs from the audience, Katt Williams acknowledged that he was truly offended by this. The fact is, this "roast" of Flava Flav seemed more like a thinly-veiled pass to be racist and offensive.

Dark-skinned African Americans also complain that they get fewer Hollywood roles, and oftentimes, a dark-skinned leading lady like Lupita Nyongo (*12 Years a Slave*) makes national and international news because people are so used to leading roles going to lighter-skinned females. Just recently, actress Zoe Saldano took on the role of Nina Simone. She also took on a boatload of criticism. It is not that African Americans feel Saldano cannot act; it's that Nina Simone fans say they cannot understand why a darker-skinned actress who looks more like Nina couldn't have been chosen for the role.

Actress Viola Davis (*How to Get Away With Murder*) says that "when you do see a woman of color onscreen, the paper-bag test is still very much alive and kicking...If you are darker than a paper bag, then you are not sexy, you are not a woman, you shouldn't be in the realm of anything that men should desire. And in the history of television and even in film, I've never seen a character like Annalise Keating (Davis' character) played by someone who looks like me: my age, my hue, my sex."[14]

It is important to note, too, that light-skinned African Americans are also ostracized and hated for no other reason than that they are light-skinned. Many report walking into a room and being immediately sized up and judged as being "stuck-up, uppity, arrogant and conceited." Many say they are hated on, scrutinized, shunned and accused of thinking they are more than their darker counter-parts—all before their accuser(s) ever bother to get to know them, even when they have done nothing more than simply show up in their lighter skin. Like their darker counter-parts, they are called names like "high yellow," "redbone," "white girl," "token," and many others.

For these and many other reasons, African Americans need to understand the importance of self-identify. We already understand that African Americans come in a wide variety of shapes and hues, and that we sport a variety of hair types and textures, nose sizes and the like; however, we must all learn to accept these differences within our communities, and this acceptance should begin with our children.

---

[14] Viola Davis on being a dark-skin black woman in Hollywood: 'The paper bag test is still alive.' TheGrio.com. June 26, 2015. http://thegrio.com/2015/06/26/viola-davis-hollywood-stereotypes-paper-bag-test/. Retrieved January 11, 2016.

Our children should understand and identify with the African American race instead of growing up to discrimirate like the older generation, or instead of wondering if African Americans are a new race of people. When we, the parents/older generation hear them ask whether we are a new race of people, we must address it. Because until our children understand who they (and we) are, there will continue to be an internal power struggle; there will continue to be internalized racism. And by the time they do discover just how unique we all are as African Americans it may well be too late. Our children may already have acted out in such a manner that they're now a part of the prison system.

We want to reach them long before this happens.

The Art of Dismissal

Accepting accountability for our own failures and our own internalized racism is an important step toward improving our African American community. However, this accountability does not mean that Blacks and Blacks alone are the cause of the problems in our communities. Nothing could be further from the truth. The fact is, whites attitudes, white actions and white racism are the cause of many of the issues in African American culture.

This negative influence began during and just after the time that Blacks were being kidnapped and re-settled in America. Blacks were stripped of their families, their property, their resources, their security, their climate, their environment, their food, their language— and perhaps most important of all, their freedom. But this forced transplantation wasn't the last time that the white man's negative actions adversely affected the African American community.

There are almost too many instances of extreme violence, destruction and even murder, to list in this one volume. However, I can offer a few examples. One incidence was the storming of

Rosewood, Florida on New Year's Day in 1923, during which time an undocumented number of African Americans were murdered. Another was the destruction of Black Wall Street (Greenwood, Oklahoma—a suburb of Tulsa, Oklahoma) two years earlier on May 31 through June 1, 1921, when as many as 300 African Americans were murdered.

In both instances, a white woman accused a Black man of sexual assault or rape, and this was all white men needed to storm the towns, burn homes, torture and kill the innocent, and run Black people off of their own property and out of their own towns. In both instances people were killed, property was stolen or completely destroyed, and innocent lives were ruined, but no one was immediately held accountable. Accountability was discussed at much later dates, but full reparations were never made. In other words, it was as if the incidents never happened.

According to the article "The Destruction of Black Wall Street" by Josie Pickens, "It was pure envy, and a vow to put progressive, high-achieving African Americans in their place that would cause the demise of the Black Mecca many called "Little Africa," and its destruction began the way much terrorism, violence and dispossession against African Americans did during that era..."[15]

Again, very little was done to rectify either of these tragedies. In the case of Rosewood, "the initial report of the Rosewood incident presented less than a month after the massacre claimed that there was insufficient evidence for prosecution." Only after renewed interest sprang up years later in 1994 (which eventually led to the 1997 movie called Rosewood by John Singleton) did the Florida legislature make reparations. And as for the destruction of The Black Wall Street, Dexter Mullins of AlJazeera wrote on July 19, 2014 that "there are

---

[15] Pickens, Josie. "The Destruction of Black Wall Street." Ebony.com. May 31, 2013. http://www.ebony.com/black-history/the-destruction-of-black-wall-street-405#axzz3wyW42HIL. Retrieved on January 11, 2016.

fewer than a dozen survivors of the riot and they will all probably die without being compensated. All city officials have offered them thus far are empty apologies."[16]

These incidents have been dismissed, just as so many other incidences, insults, tragedies and wrongdoings perpetrated by the white man upon the Black community. Whites have historically been dismissive of issues they have caused in our culture. Even when we as a people made a come-back in the time of Dr. Martin Luther King, Jr., we still lost it all because of them.

These incidences have caused a snowball effect of negativity and have left the bulk of African American communities in a time loop of calamitous serendipity. And yet even with all the evidence of their own contributions to the problems right under their noses, white people act as if they cannot figure out what is wrong in the African American communities. They are very aware of the issues but prefer to play the game of not understanding why Blacks can't seem to get ahead or "make it." They do not understand because of ignorance, blindness, denial, or because they simply find it easier to play the blame game.

In the meantime, whites continue to look at African Americans as if they are monkeys in the bush. As long as African Americans scrape by on scraps, whites can tolerate their presence. This tolerance happens only if African Americans worship whites like they are God and don't surpass them in any way. For example, when an African American surpasses a white person in a sport or earns more money than a white person, that white person would rather kill him- or herself—or *you*—than to accept and admit that you are doing better than him or her. This is because they have been told all their lives that they are superior to African Americans and they cannot make

---

[16] Mullins, Dexter. "Survivors of Infamous 1921 Tulsa Race Riot Still Hope for Justice." Aljazeera America. Aljazeera.com. http://america.aljazeera.com/articles/2014/7/19/survivors-of-infamous1921tulsaraceriotstillhopeforjustice.html. Retrieved January 11, 2016.

themselves accept that anything an African American might do, say or become would equal or surpass what they do.

It is for these reasons that even when an African American has shown him- or herself superior in a certain area, whites still typically speak to him or her in a condescending manner, saying things like, "You're not like most African Americans," or "You're smart for a Black person," or "You're a credit to your race." And it is also for these reasons that when a white person sees that a Black person is doing "better than they should be" and are almost there, they will throw something—*anything,* in that Black person's path to stop them.

Is the white race the only race that dismisses the struggles and issues of Black Americans? Not at all. Take the case of rookie NYPD (New York City Police) Officer Peter Liang who was recently convicted of the second-degree manslaughter of an unarmed Black man named Akai Gurley. Liang and his partner were patrolling a Brooklyn housing project when Liang claims he was startled by a sound and fired his gun as a reflex. The bullet ricocheted off a wall and hit Gurley as he was walking on the floor just below where the officers patrolled.

By the time Liang and his partner arrived on the scene, Gurley's girlfriend was trying to revive him. Liang never offered assistance because "he was in shock and felt unqualified to perform CPR due to inadequate training,"[17] according to his lawyer. So, in addition to the second degree manslaughter charges, Liang was also charged with official misconduct and currently faces 15 years in prison.

Immediately following Liang's conviction, protests sprang up everywhere: "an estimated 5,000 people marched in downtown Philadelphia and thousands more rallied in San Francisco and Los Angeles's Chinatown, and other protests occurred at the Washington

---

[17] Ax, Joseph. "NY Policeman Guilty of Manslaughter in Shooting of Unarmed Black Man." Reuters. February 12, 2016. http://www.reuters.com/article/us-new-york-police-idUSKCN0VL01X. Retrieved on March 1, 2016.

Monument and in Boston, Chicago, Dallas, Denver and Miami.[18] The protesters claimed that "this is an issue affecting the country's Asian-American community."[19]

James Wilkinson of the Daily Mail wrote that a crowd of 15,000 people marched just outside the federal courthouse in Brooklyn, citing 'scapegoating' and 'selective justice' in Liang's case, and insisting that his conviction "only occurred because he [Liang] is a minority, and that it was intended to pacify those who are angry about other shootings of minorities by police in the US, which has been a hot topic over the past year."[20] One protester even held up a sign with Dr. Martin Luther King, Jr.'s face and the words "Dream for all Americans."

In short, many of these activists see the Liang verdict as racial inequality and feel that "Liang's trial [is] a counterweight to cases in which grand juries have declined to indict officers, including the cases of Michael Brown in Missouri and Eric Garner in New York."[21]

This situation would be laughable if it wasn't so serious. Other races hardly ever speak up when they see the things that are said and done to African Americans. Unless and until they get their own taste of "white supremacy" they just don't feel that our struggle is real. Oh, they may see that what we are experiencing is wrong, but they don't bother to speak up. They never say a word, except possibly to wonder aloud why Blacks "can't seem to make it." But when the shoe is on the other foot and *they* experience discrimination—when *they* suddenly

---

[18] Wilkinson, James. "Nearly 15k People Protest in New York over Asian-American Cop's Manslaughter Conviction For Shooting Unarmed Black Man." DailyMail.com. February 21, 2016. http://www.dailymail.co.uk/news/article-3456387/Thousands-rally-NYC-US-officers-conviction.html. Retrieved on March 1, 2016.
[19] Ibid.
[20] Wilkinson, James. "Nearly 15k People Protest in New York over Asian-American Cop's Manslaughter Conviction For Shooting Unarmed Black Man." DailyMail.com. February 21, 2016. http://www.dailymail.co.uk/news/article-3456387/Thousands-rally-NYC-US-officers-conviction.html. Retrieved on March 1, 2016.
[21] Ibid.

discover that whites consider them a minority, too—then and only then do they decide to yell discrimination.

Is it discrimination when a white cop is acquitted for killing an unarmed Black man while an Asian-American cop who commits the same act is found guilty? Possibly. In the meantime, welcome to the Black man's world. We have been dealing with this type of discrimination for over 400 years.

CHAPTER 3

It's a Setup

A frican Americans have been set up to fail almost from the very beginning. I say "almost" because when Blacks first came to America in 1619, things were different. Those African Americans were indentured servants and were expected to work from four to seven years to earn their freedom.

What went wrong? The problem for early settlers (and ultimately for the African Americans) was that the settlers had lots of land and no one to work it, and paying indentured servants was growing more and more expensive. Eventually, owning slaves became a profitable business and slavery became the norm.

This, admittedly, is a watered-down version of how slavery came to be, but you get the idea. And by now, everyone knows the basic story of slavery; how slaves were worked, misused, violated, raped, exploited, murdered, sold away, and made to feel and behave as if they were inferior to whites.

When freedom came in the mid-1860's and whites no longer "owned" African Americans, a series of written and unwritten laws (including segregation and the Jim Crow laws) were enforced to keep

African Americans in their *un*-equal place in society. But even after the Jim Crow laws were done away with, the system was carefully and methodically set up to make sure that African Americans failed across the board.

In the early days, the education system for African Americans was markedly unequal to that of whites. African Americans had inferior schools, inferior supplies, inferior and outdated books, and no clear understanding of their own true history. Only the white man's version of history was written into the history books.

The same goes for the medical history of African Americans. In the late 1800s and early 1900s, African Americans were not typically allowed in white hospitals, and white doctors and nurses did not want to have anything to do with them. African Americans suffered greatly because of this. African American doctors who graduated from such medical colleges as Meharry Medical College and Howard University College of Medicine often built and operated hospitals of their own that opened their doors and their hospital beds to the Black community.

After desegregation, things should have been on the upswing; however, another system was put into place to keep African Americans oppressed, ignorant and MIA (missing in action) from their own families and neighborhoods: the prison system. According to ABC news, "the US has five percent (5%) of the world's population but a quarter of the world's prisoners, with over 2.3 million people behind bars, dwarfing other nations. The US rate of incarceration is five to eight times higher than other highly developed countries and Black males are the largest percentage of inmates.[22]

---

[22] Quigley, Bill. "Fourteen Examples of Racism in Criminal Justice System." HuffingtonPost.com. http://www.huffingtonpost.com/bill-quigley/fourteen-examples-of-raci_b_658947.html. Retrieved January 12, 2016.

The ACLU conducted a study that found that "Blacks are three times more likely to be stopped [by the police] than whites,[23] and that once arrested, they "are more likely to remain in prison awaiting trial than whites.[24] In the meantime, it is said that most African Americans defendants never get a trial and "most plea bargains consist of the promise of a longer sentence if a person exercises their constitutional right to trial.[25]

Those African Americans who do go to trial are likely not to have many (or any) African Americans on the jury. In 2010, the Equal Justice Initiative found that "African Americans are frequently illegally excluded from criminal jury service.[26] Unfortunately, the bad news does not end there. The U.S. Sentencing Commission reports that "in the federal system, Black offenders receive sentences that are 10% longer than white offenders for the same crimes[27] so that though "African Americans make up 13% of the population and 14% of drug users, they are not only 37% of the people arrested for drugs, but 56% of the people in state prisons for drug offenses.[28]

What does this all mean? The US Bureau of Justice Statistics explains it by writing that "the chance of a Black male born in 2001 of going to jail is 32%, or 1 in three. Latino males have a 17% chance [of going to jail] and white males have a 6% chance. Thus, Black boys are five times and Latino boys are nearly three times as likely as white boys to go to jail.[29] African American juvenile youth make up only 16% of the population, yet they make up at least 28% of juvenile arrests,

[23] Quigley, Bill. "Fourteen Examples of Racism in Criminal Justice System." HuffingtonPost.com. http://www.huffingtonpost.com/bill-quigley/fourteen-examples-of-raci_b_658947.html. Retrieved January 12, 2016.
[24] Quigley, Bill. Ibid.
[25] Quigley, Bill. Ibid
[26] Quigley, Bill. Ibid
[27] Quigley, Bill. Ibid
[28] Quigley, Bill. Ibid.
[29] Quigley, Bill. Ibid.

37% of the total number of youth in juvenile jails, and 58% of the youth sent to adult prisons. (2009 Criminal Justice Primer, The Sentencing Project).[30]

If these young men do ever make it out of the prison system, the odds of finding a job and trying to build a semblance of a normal life are slim. In fact, when white criminals and African American criminals exit the prison system and apply for jobs, "17% of white job applicants with criminal records receive call backs from employers while only 5% of Black job applicants with criminal records receive call backs. (Professor Devah Pager of the University of Wisconsin)[31]

With such bleak statistics as these, it is obvious that the laws of the land were not designed to protect African Americans; they were not developed so that African Americans could live equivocally or comfortably, but basically so that they can be "contained" through such methods as imposing longer sentences for the same or lesser charges than their white counterparts. One comparison is the case of football quarterback Michael Vick, who was convicted of running an illegal dog fighting ring. He was sentenced to 23 months in prison, was suspended without pay from the NFL, and lost all of his endorsements.

That was in 2007. Today Vick is still called an evil animal abuser. Compare his case to 21-year old Dylan Roof, the white man who walked into a Black church and gunned down nine worshippers during a bible study meeting. His defense lawyers had every intention of pulling the "insanity" card so that they could have him labeled as mentally ill; however, Roof's admission to the surviving worshippers that he was trying to start a race war knocked that defense off the

---

[30] Quigley, Bill. "Fourteen Examples of Racism in Criminal Justice System." HuffingtonPost.com.http://www.huffingtonpost.com/bill-quigley/fourteen-examples-of-raci_b_658947.html. Retrieved January 12, 2016.
[31] Quigley, Bill. Ibid.

table. It is rumored that his team now plans to use the "he was bullied and ridiculed all his life" defense to help him avoid the death penalty and reduce some of his jail time.

One man was stripped of everything because he allowed one dog to fight another, and one man walked into a church and shot down nine people in cold blood and his lawyers are going to pull out all the stops to get him off. Now, I'm not saying that what Michael Vick did is acceptable; I am saying that African Americans are given harsher sentences than their white counterparts.

The prison system is simply not designed to rehabilitate African Americans; it's designed to incarcerate them so long that they are forgotten by society. Money *is* invested in the prison system, but it is not invested to get these misguided men back on track. It is invested because the prison system is a multi-billion dollar business and there's profit to be had by those who run it.

CHAPTER 4

Dissention in the Camp

So far we have discussed many of the *outside* forces that have influenced the Black community, but it is important to note that there are many *inside* forces that have a crushing influence on our community, too.

The Prostitution of Civil Rights

Long after the Civil War ended, African Americans were still living in a land of oppression, segregation, hatred and uncertainty. There was stark racism, separatism, obvious inequality, and even violence all around, and the Civil Rights movement sprang forth out of necessity and sheer determination.

I won't attempt to go into a thorough lesson about the Civil Rights movement and all that it entailed (and still entails; the struggle continues!), because I would need to write many books to do so. If you want to know more about the Civil Rights movement, you can launch a search in your favorite search engine on any given day and come up with hundreds of websites that give you a blow-by-blow about what happened, what resulted, and where we are now. For purposes of this book, I simply want to emphasize how, in my opinion, the Civil Rights movement continues to influence the African American community.

Many Civil Rights leaders prostitute our civil rights by blaming absolutely everything on the white man. That includes poverty, joblessness, out-of-wedlock births, Black-on-Black killings, negative mindsets—you name it and it's the white man's fault, according to them. Now, notice that I said "many" and not "all," because we do have some powerful and effective Civil Rights leaders out there, like famed academic, activist and philosopher, Cornel West; Certified School Psychologist and blood relative of Frederick Douglass, Dr. Umar Johnson; American academic, author, and radio host, Professor Michael Eric Dyson; and American civil rights activist, social critic, writer, entrepreneur, and comedian Dick Gregory. But the majority of so-called civil rights leaders often convey to the world *and* the African American community that "nothing is our fault; it wouldn't have happened if the white man hadn't been behind it."

There's no unity, no camaraderie among our civil rights leaders. A USA Today article called *"Civil Rights Leaders at Odds as Ferguson Protests Grow,"* by Yamiche Alcindor, talks about the "growing tensions between longstanding civil rights groups that have battled discrimination for decades and new groups of leaders who want an edgier approach."[32] These activists who protested and marched after the Ferguson incident want their opportunity to voice their interests and demands and feel they're just as entitled to be heard as "old heads" like Al Sharpton and the NAACP. The article goes on to state that even though these newer activists "may share goals with more experienced groups, they have clashed with them in attempts at joint efforts."[33]

---

[32] Alcindor, Yamiche. "Civil Rights Leaders at Odds as Ferguson Protests Grow." USA Today. USAToday.com. http://www.usatoday.com/story/news/nation/2014/12/28/as-ferguson-protest-grows-so-do-tensions/20664395/. Retrieved January 16, 2016.

One prominent example is when Rev. Al Sharpton organized a March in Washington, DC (December 13, 2014) and some of the younger activists from the Ferguson protest pushed their way onto the stage and said, "This movement was started by the young people. We started this. There should be young people all over this stage. This should be young people all up here."[34]

According to the article, this was actually the second time that younger activists had disrespected the elder activists and demanded a piece of the spotlight. As a result "several clergy members ceded their spots to protesters, who told the crowd that NAACP President Cornell William Brooks was out of touch."[35] The young activists went on to say that "this ain't your grandparents' civil rights movement. A lot of us are not scholars. We're not trained organizers. We are not professional activists. We are just real people who identified a problem and decided to do something about it."[36]

The fact that young people want to be bolder and more daring isn't a bad thing, but the way they are going about it is disrespectful, divisive, embarrassing, and generally confusing for the masses. The African American community needs real leaders, but if the leaders are all shoving each other aside, who should we listen to?

And they are not the only problem. This type of dissention and lack of unity has been around a long time. Rep. John Lewis (D-Ga) was the youngest speaker at the 1963 march on Washington, and he recalls how Thurgood Marshall, one time head of the NAACP Legal Defense Fund "criticized the group for staging sit-ins at segregated

---

[33] Alcindor, Yamiche. "Civil Rights Leaders at Odds as Ferguson Protests Grow." USA Today. USAToday.com. http://www.usatoday.com/story/news/nation/2014/12/28/as-ferguson-protest-grows-so-do-tensions/20664395/. Retrieved January 16, 2015.

[34] Ibid. Direct quote of Johnetta Elzie of St. Louis.

[35] Alcindor, Yamiche. "Civil Rights Leaders at Odds as Ferguson Protests Grow." USA Today. USAToday.com.http://www.usatoday.com/story/news/nation/2014/12/28/as-ferguson-protest-grows-so-do-tensions/20664395/. Retrieved January 16, 2015.

[36] Ibid. Direct quote of rapper and activist Tef Poe.

lunch counters that led to arrests and beatings by whites angered at their presence. Marshall instead favored litigating for civil rights in the courts."[37] Rep. Lewis' reply to Marshall was ""We need a mass movement. That's why we go on the freedom rides, that's why we sit-in, that's why we continue to march."[38] Lewis still feels that way today. Conversely, Al Sharpton doesn't agree. He criticized the protestors for their "arrogant approach that disrespects the decades of protest work he and civil rights leaders have done."[39]

Confusion of any type is not good for a movement...or a community. But confusion of this type is sure to tear the African American community apart, because it is no longer the community against the system of oppression. It is the leaders of the community against themselves.

The Blame Game

I could say a lot about the blame game, but instead I want to post a moving, timely and relevant opinion by Pastor (Dr.) Tony Evans which I feel reveals who or what is really to blame for the African American community's downward spiral and eventual demise if we don't turn things around.

These are excerpts from Pastor Evans' interview with Dr. Darrel Bock (Executive Director for Cultural Engagement, Dallas Theological Seminary) about the topic of "Racial Reconciliation and the Church."[40]

---

[37] Alcindor, Yamiche. "Civil Rights Leaders at Odds as Ferguson Protests Grow." USA Today. USAToday.com.http://www.usatoday.com/story/news/nation/2014/12/28/as-ferguson-protest-grows-so-do-tensions/20664395/. Retrieved January 16, 2016.

[37] Ibid. Direct quote of rapper and activist Tef Poe.

[38] Ibid

[39] Ibid.

[40]Bock, Dr. Darrell. Racial Reconciliation and the Church. Dallas Theological Seminary. Retrieved on January 16, 2016. http://www.dts.edu/thetable/play/racial-reconciliation-and-church/#transcript

"...the biggest problem in Black America today is the breakdown of the family. The breakdown of the family is unraveling us as a community. When 70 percent plus of your children are being born out of wedlock and the fathers are not there to tend to them, you've got chaos in the community. That's crime, that's unemployment and most of these kids are going to be raised in poverty. So and that's something we control. That's something we control.

The White man is not making you do that. He's not forcing you into that position. That's a convenient "out". In slavery when we did not have laws on our side, the community on our side, the government on our side, the broader   community on our side, our families were a lot stronger. We were a lot more unified and we made a lot more progress. We're going through regression right now and a lot of that is because of decision-making we are responsible for."[41]

And then there is that stinging but not completely off-the-mark speech by Bill Cosby called *We Can't Blame White People.* Here are only a couple of excerpts that help to clarify just who, exactly, is responsible for the problems in the African American community:

"They're standing on the corner and they can't speak English. I can't even talk the way these people talk:

'Why you ain't, Where you is, What he drive, Where he stay, Where he work, Who you be...' And I blamed the kid until I heard the mother talk. And then I heard the father talk. Brown or Black versus the Board of Education is no longer the white person's problem. We have got to take the neighborhood back. People used to be ashamed. Today a woman has eight children with eight different 'husbands' — or men or whatever you call them now. We have millionaire football players who cannot read. We have million-dollar basketball players who can't write two paragraphs. We as black folks have to do a better job. Someone working at Walmart with seven kids, you are hurting us. We have to start holding each other to a higher standard." We cannot blame the white people any longer. [42]

---

[41] Ibid.

I'll let you draw your own conclusions from these two excerpts, and I will only add this: We cannot continue to go around blaming other races because we aren't successful or because we aren't putting food into our own mouths. We cannot continue to blame other races because we're not advancing when at least 70% of the time the problem is that we're just being lazy.

We're not reading books, we're not asking for knowledge, and we're certainly not seeking it. We're not looking for information and we're not traveling abroad to open our minds and learn about other cultures.

Until we begin to address these monumental tasks—or at least begin with the smallest tasks among them, we cannot point the finger at anyone except ourselves.

We Don't Support Our Own

The dollar once "circulated 36 to 100 times [in the Black community], sometimes taking a year for currency to leave the community. Now a dollar leaves the Black community in 15 minutes."[43] What happened? Did it all go downhill because of one or two tragedies like the destruction of Black Wall Street or the massacre at Rosewood...or is there something more going on?

The truth is that African Americans don't support Black businesses and they don't support each other, either. While African Americans are focusing their whole minds on identifying the people who are being racist toward them or discriminating against them or

---

[42] Cos Cause. From "We Can't Blame White People."Snopes.com. Retrieved January 16, 2016. http://www.snopes.com/politics/soapbox/cosby.asp

[43] "What Happened to Black Wall Street on June 1, 1921?" Bay View. Sfbayview.com. February 9, 2011. http://sfbayview.com/2011/02/what-happened-to-black-wall-street-on-june-1-1921/. Retrieved January 16, 2016.

oppressing them in some way, they do not even recognize that *they* are actually more racist toward each other than any other race could ever be.

Author Lawrence M. Watkins of The Grio wrote an article called "4 half-truths about black-owned businesses — and why you should still buy black," and he identified some pretty disheartening but true reasons that African Americans do not support our own businesses. These reasons include:

1) Insisting that customer service is extremely poor.
2) Claiming the prices are higher than every other store's prices.
3) Claiming that encouraging people to buy black is racist.
4) Claiming black businesses don't have any products that black people want to buy.[44]

These myths can, of course, be dispelled. For one thing, customer service in Black businesses has not proven to be worse than in white businesses; it just seems to be remembered longer and not forgiven more in Black businesses. Prices in Black businesses often are higher than in their white counterparts, but this is largely due to the fact that "Blacks do not typically control their own value chains."[45] For example, Black hair salons are charged higher rates from suppliers because people from other cultures often own the raw materials and means of production that go into having a nice hair-do.[46]

---

[44] Watkins, Lawrence M. "4 half-truths about black-owned businesses — and why you should still buy blac." The Grio. TheGrio.com. http://thegrio.com/2012/07/23/4-half-truths-about-black-owned-businesses-and-why-you-should-still-buy-black/. Retrieved January 19, 2016.

[45] Watkins, Lawrence M. "4 half-truths about black-owned businesses — and why you should still buy blac." The Grio. TheGrio.com. http://thegrio.com/2012/07/23/4-half-truths-about-black-owned-businesses-and-why-you-should-still-buy-black/. Retrieved January 19, 2016.

[46] Ibid.

Some African Americans feel that the only way for Black people to succeed is to not be seen as "Black" but as Americans. Therefore, they advocate "buying American" and not necessarily "buying Black." And as for not offering products that other African Americans want to buy, author Lawrence Watkins says that "because some businesses have a higher cost of entry and Blacks have a harder time acquiring the necessary capital to compete, our community just doesn't offer a huge array of products and services [other than the hair care/beauty, jewelry, or food markets] — at least for now.[47]

In the meantime, African Americans have accepted European ideology—which basically means that "white ice is colder than Black ice," "white products are superior to Black products," and "white is right." African Americans look toward the white man and the European culture to determine what is good or bad and think that other African Americans don't have a clue what business is, how to run one, or how to serve others.

African Americans rush off to schools that teach them the European way of thinking, acting, presenting, doing business and treating others. These are schools that offer them a *European* degree after they have finished their training. African Americans then rush out with these degrees and land jobs wherein they begin building someone else's empire. They do not create legacies of their own.

Think about it: the majority of these European ideology schools teach African Americans how to dress to impress employers, how to interview well, how to be good employees, how to hold onto their jobs, and how to earn wealth for their employers. But these schools neglect to emphasize those skills needed to think outside the box; to find a need in society and then go about fulfilling that need via entrepreneurial activities and purpose. These schools do not teach

---

[47] Ibid.

African Americans how to organize a business, fundraise, market, import and export (if necessary), hone a product, and advertise to grow their own business. They only teach African Americans how to use their backs and their minds to create a lasting legacy for someone else.

Excuses and Entitlement

Leadership problems and lack of support in the Black business sector aren't our only issues. There is also the huge problem of excuses, entitlement and the welfare or "dependency" culture. According to the article *"The Decline of the African American Family"*[48] by Dean Kalahar, "we must stop ignoring bad behavior and choices in the African-American community. Discriminating between proper and bad behavior [is] a legitimate judgment [and] not discrimination or bigotry."

The truth is that many years have been spent figuring out the monumental effect that slavery has had on the African American family and community. The culmination of the findings was, among other things, for whites to develop a case of "white guilt" that would lead President Lyndon B. Johnson to wage "War on Poverty" by implementing a number of entitlement programs.[49] Before these entitlements, "examples of a vibrant Black family institution in America's [were] too numerous to ignore,"[50] like the fact that in 1950, 72% of all Black men and 81% of Black women had been married; prior to the 1960's, the unemployment rate for Black 16- and 17-year olds was under 10%; before 1960, both poverty and dependency were

---

[48] Kalahar, Dean. "The Decline of the African American Family." AmericanThinker.com, http://www.americanthinker.com/articles/2014/03/the_decline_of_the_africanamerican_famil y.html. Retrieved on January 20, 2016.

[49] Kalahar, Dean. "The Decline of the African American Family." AmericanThinker.com, http://www.americanthinker.com/articles/2014/03/the_decline_of_the_africanamerican_famil y.html. Retrieved on January 20, 2016.

[50] Ibid.

declining and Black income was rising in both absolute and relative terms to white income; and by 1965, 76.4% of Black children were born to married women."[51]

Then the white guilt prevailed, behavioral judgment of African Americans was largely frowned upon (according to the Kalahar article), and "the cultural glue that held together the African-American family was fundamentally changed [and] this destabilization has created turbulent neighborhoods that have devastating costs to children ranging from poverty, educational deficiencies, violence, crime, drugs, and a culture of victimization and entitlement."[52]

The result is a type of hybrid culture that is lacking in accountability, responsibility, proper and consistent parenting, pursuit of education, love of self and community, and building of personal and community legacies. In other words, the fact that welfare is in place and is accessible to those who need it is no reason not to aspire to get to a point where it is no longer needed. The fact that free housing is available is no reason to decide you're going to be there forever because you want to keep your money in your pocket; and the fact that a free education is promised to all does not mean that teachers and support persons can be abused, rebelled against, beaten or ignored at your whim.

African Americans must begin to see the value in their communities, their support people, their children and their aspirations. This includes taking parenting seriously, learning to commit to healthy and permanent relationships with members of the opposite sex (within our communities), valuing education and the teachers who pass on knowledge and understanding, and learning to articulate feelings, beliefs and opinions in a clear and respectable

---

[51] Ibid.
[52] Ibid.

manner. It also means ceasing to ostracize those African Americans who are not the same shade of Black or brown that we are, who do not speak as we do, or who have more (or less) of an education than we do.

CHAPTER 5

The Media and Why We're Not Making It

H ow does the African American community begin learning to love itself and plan lasting legacies for the families within the community? First we must recognize that there truly is a problem, and then we must find the problem's exact location so we can isolate it and eventually wipe it out.

One of the biggest problems in the African American community is the issue of what has become of the Black woman. The fact is that Black women have been bamboozled. That's right, they have been tricked first-hand and the present-day status of the African American community is what they (and we all) have to show for it.

I am in no wise blaming everything on the Black woman because the Black man certainly has his faults. I emphasize the Black woman because she is the glue that holds the entire family together. She is the one who encourages her man, nurtures her children, manages the household, prepares the meals, and even works out in the world to bring in needed income—even if her man works, too. And whenever any Black man walks away from his home and family for whatever reason, the Black woman is typically the one still cradling the children, still nurturing, still carving out a way for the family to survive.

So for purposes of this chapter, I'll emphasize the major problems plaguing today's Black woman.

The Curse of the Media

There was a time when there were very few African American women on television. Our "sheroes" were the Prissy's and the Mammy's of the early TV days. Not to say there was anything wrong with these women's performances; they took the roles that were available to them at the time and did their best with them. But this was what we had. We saw air-heads or babbling, overweight cooks, or the occasional over-sexed jezebel that enticed men to have sex with them.

Then came the 1960's and Star Trek's Lieutenant Nyota Uhura (Nichelle Nichols), who was smart, beautiful, classy, sassy, and absolutely necessary for the well-being of the Starship Enterprise. But the Lieutenant Uhura's were (and still are) few and far between. Today we see bickering, back-biting, back-stabbing women like the Basketball Wives of LA who seem to be popular because they are merciless, mercenary divas who are in a rollercoaster love/hate relationship with their men and each other, and who will snatch off those earrings and fight at the drop of a dime.

Another example is celebrity Omarosa Manigault, who was a contestant on the first season of Donald Trump's *The Apprentice*. Omarosa's tactics have been called "controversial, blindsiding, alienatory, and acrimonious,"[53] yet she was quickly embraced as the woman America loved to hate.

The media, it seems, loves the "angry Black woman." They love this image so much that in many subliminal ways they insinuate that a Black woman isn't a true Black woman unless she's angry, volatile, unpredictable, snarky, and condescending toward everyone within earshot—especially other Black women. A 2013 Huffington Post article by Rhonesha Byng states that an *Essence* survey of Black women in the media revealed that Black women are typically portrayed as "Gold Diggers, Modern Jezebels, Baby Mamas, Uneducated Sisters, Ratchet Women, Angry Black Women, Mean Black Girls, Unhealthy Black Women, and Black Barbies."[54]

This can be further validated simply by noting several celebrated African American female characters in well-known movies:

1. Whoopi Goldberg played a con woman and phony psychic in *Ghost*.
2. Halle Berry played an abusive mother in *Monster's Ball*.
3. Mo'Nique played an abusive mother in *Precious*.
4. Octavia Spencer played a chicken-frying maid in *The Help*.
5. Hattie McDaniel played a blustering "Mammy" in *Gone With the Wind*.
6. Lupita Nyong'o played the raped, humiliated and victimized slave in *12 Years a Slave*.

In these movies, the African American female's character is brash and abusive with zero parenting skills, or a downright liar, or a con woman, or a slave at the whim of her lustful master/mistress, or a maid with out-of-this-world cooking skills whose only function is to fry chicken and serve others.

---

[53] Wikipedia, the Free Dictionary. https://en.wikipedia.org/wiki/Omarosa. Retrieved January 20, 2016.

[54] Byng, Rhonesha. The Images of Black Women in the Media 'Stil Only Scratch the Surface', EssenceStudy Finds." HuffingtonPost.com. http://www.huffingtonpost.com/2013/10/15/the-images-of-black-women-in-media_n_4102322.html. Retrieved January 20, 2016.

Fake. Just Fake.

These aren't the only qualities the media seems to dump on our Black women. It also dumps the myth that the Black woman is not beautiful if she doesn't have "long hair, long nails, a big butt and a haughty, *I'll-kick-your-ass* attitude." Unfortunately, Black women rush to comply. Black women buy fake eyelashes, fake eyebrows, and fake eye contacts. They are not above booty-injections to make their behinds even rounder and more noticeable; and if they cannot afford a medically-induced behind, they do the next best thing and wear a fake booty.

Yes, white women and women of other races do this, too, but right now we're talking about the women in *our* communities. We're talking about a culture where our little girls grow up thinking they must have the biggest butt on the block or they'll be considered pretty much useless. We're talking about a culture where girls and women by the thousands rush to concerts where men sing songs like "Back That Ass Up"—and these girls take their young children along with them. We're talking about a culture where songs like *Anaconda* top the charts and contests to find the best (and raunchiest) twerkers are the "in" things to participate in.

We're talking about a culture where our women no longer feel comfortable in their own skin, but rather strive to look like the women of other cultures to attract men. They don't even understand that a real Black man doesn't want them simply because they *are* so fake. A real man will say, "Why should I want you? You're not even a real woman."

I'll say it again: the Black woman has been bamboozled--and this "bamboozling" didn't just happen on its own; Black men have a lot to do with it. Black men have unrealistic expectations for Black women. They want their booties to be huge, their waists to be small, their breasts to be humongous, and their sexual appetite to be out of this world. They expect the Black woman to do whatever it takes to give them the body they're looking for, even to her own destruction.

Does the Black man hold women of other races to this standard? Think about it: a Black man will hold hands with an obese white woman as they take a pleasant "lover's" stroll through the park, and he will treat her like the queen of his life. *In front of everyone!* Yet this same Black man will typically hesitate being seen in public with a fat Black woman. He may cavort with her at night behind closed doors, but in the day time he will act as if he doesn't know her. During daylight hours, he has a certain standard he wants to project, and the Black woman must meet or exceed that standard.

By the same token, many Black men are now going so far as to insist that Black women bring a certain amount of money and substance to the table in a relationship. Many Black men fully expect the Black woman to pay their bills, buy their clothes, take them on vacation, and take care of them. And it is no secret that many Black men make a practice out of seeing how many Black women they can "collect" simply because they know these women are lonely and are craving love and attention.

Sadly, Black women accept these games and they—and the children that result from these encounters--are the ones to suffer for it. By the time many of these women have matured enough to know that they are throwing away their bodies and their lives, they already have two or three illegitimate children by as many fathers and seem to be truly surprised that no decent Black man wants to marry them.

Gay and Effeminate Men

One last issue that goes along with the plight of the Black woman is the issue of gay and effeminate Black men. The truth is that Black men are becoming so much more effeminate that Black women are starting to take on more masculine tendencies. They don't necessarily do this because they want to, either. They do it because they have to.

Black women are enabling Black men to be effeminate. How? A woman who provides for and takes care of a man shouldn't consider that man a true man. And she definitely shouldn't consider him as companion material. In fact, he should be the fish that she tosses back into the sea. But that is not what's happening today. Today's Black women are enabling the destructive behavior of Black men by thinking that if caring for and providing for a Black man is what it takes to get and keep a Black man, then that's what she's going to do.

Let me be clear: I'm not putting down men who are not currently in a position to provide for a woman. A man who cannot provide for a woman isn't necessarily a bad man; it just means that for whatever reason, he's just not ready. His issue could be medical, social, or educational. Maybe he is focusing on getting a degree or starting and expanding a business before he is ready to take on the responsibility of a woman and a future family. But when a woman encounters a man who cannot provide for her and she has no problem taking care of and providing for him, that's a problem.

Men have become so effeminate that they have lost their place in today's society. The characteristics of being a provider, protector and leader are gone; in their place is a man who allows his woman to work the job, bring home the money, buy the food, make the decisions, and run the household. A lot of our Black men have become lazy, soft and easily intimidated. In fact, the best word to describe them is "domesticated." Yes, these men are domesticated.

Here's an example: a lion is a hunter. A lion rules. But when you take that lion from the jungle and domesticate it and then later try to return it to the jungle, that lion has no clue what to do. It has become accustomed to being fed and housed. It has become accustomed to not having to hunt for its food; not having to compete against other lions in the jungle.

That is how it is with Black men. Many have become domesticated, and unfortunately, Black women don't mind. They are enabling this behavior.

CHAPTER 6

Out of the Rabbit Hole

I t's time to climb out of the rabbit hole and African Americans will need all the tools they can get to do so. First, African Americans must take full accountability for our own actions and admit that we've made a lot of poor choices over the last 200 years. Second, we must develop some kindness, some respect, and some camaraderie toward each other. We must learn to stop lashing out at each other. We must learn to like each other and wish the best for each other. Because the way things stand, an African American will kill you first before any other race will.

Next, we need to take a look at what is actually happening around us. The world is getting smaller. Globalization is happening, and it's happening fast. The Information Highway is expanding and the world is shrinking. As a result, many countries are losing power and position because they simply don't know how to play the game anymore. That includes white Americans. They have always been told that they are the superior race; that they can out-think and out-do African Americans with hardly any effort at all. But now they are finding that this simply is not true. With globalization has come a "leveling of the playing field" so that everyone has a chance. Now white people are out there competing for the same $15 per hour jobs that African Americans and other so-called minorities are competing for.

These same whites who were once chosen first for jobs now find that the paradigms have changed and they are all but out in the cold. They have no diploma, they have no real education. They have nothing except the color of their skin, and this is no longer good enough anymore. Other races are becoming successful and this is making white people nervous. They have to compete for jobs based on knowledge and skill and not just the color of their skin, and things are getting crucial.

This fierce competition is one of the reasons that white people prefer to be condescending to blacks and other minorities when they encounter them. Even in this day and time when stereotypes should have been long ago done away with, they see an African American and clutch their purse or wallet. They shrink away, as if to say that they know you are a thief or a thug or a killer. This is their way of perpetuating the stereotype that you are a sub-par human being. It is the only thing that makes them feel better.

The fact is, in 2016 you can be any race, any gender you please, and you can succeed at whatever you choose to do or be. Think of the news stories of 2015 where a white woman chose to identify as Black. Think of all the instances where Black people chose to identify as multi-racial or "American" but not as Black. The truth is, we live in a society where practically everything goes, and white people don't like this. Many whites have fallen into poverty, and quite simply, they're struggling. All their lives they have been told that being white was the end-all of life, but now that's just not true. Now, if you are intelligent and if you have wealth or if you come from a certain family, that will get you by—even if you're not white. White people don't like this, and because they don't like it, many are doing their best to see that something—anything, holds African Americans back.

How do we get out of the rabbit hole? By understanding how we got there in the first place; by understanding what it's like inside the rabbit hole; and by understanding what's waiting for us on the other side when we finally do get out. African Americans must realize that we are in the middle of the "You-are-not-supposed-to-be-here" syndrome. We must remember that white people always knew that a certain percentage of Blacks would succeed, and they made slight accommodations for that fact. But they never planned for *all Blacks* to be on equal footing, and this has created a panic. Whites designed the system to accept only a certain amount of successful minorities and no more. In other words, they always knew that "there would always be that one [Black person] that just wouldn't go away. Therefore, they created a "built-in buffer" to deal with only a certain amount of us— typically, those of us who go to their schools, earn diplomas that they designed, and learn their ways.

African Americans can come out of the rabbit hole. There is nothing stopping us. And there is also nothing stopping us from becoming educated, buying a home, having a car, earning a six-figure salary and raising a family. There is nothing even stopping us from starting and growing a business. It can happen, all of it, but when and if it does, it will happen because we as individuals and communities have decided that we're done wasting time and are ready to get serious.

It can happen as long as we're not somewhere holding our breath and waiting for that elusive official apology for slavery, or for those wonderful financial reparations that will probably never come. Whatever successes we experience as we climb out of the rabbit hole and whatever ground we gain once we're out will be the result of our own effort, determination and mutual participation. We cannot look for any other race to pull us up or drag us to our victorious stand. We must do this for ourselves.

CHAPTER 7

The Importance of Transparency

No one wants the wool pulled over their eyes. No one wants to be told one thing and then be presented with the exact opposite. And definitely no one wants to be told that they're imagining things—or that things aren't as bad as they seem—especially when they can see what is going on for themselves. People want transparency; they crave it. People want to be "in on the truth of what's going on," even if the truth hurts.

In that light, prepare yourself. This may sting a little.

First Things First

So exactly what is "transparency?" It means when something is clear and the observer can see all the way through it. In the case of racism and bigotry, it means "calling a spade a spade" and acknowledging separatism, envy, or ill will for what they are. It is admitting that racism and hatred *do* exist, no matter how neatly people attempt to hide them or explain them away.

When I mention racism and hatred, you probably think I'm talking about the racism that the white community has shown toward African Americans as a whole, but I'm not. I'm not talking about white people at all right now. I'm talking about **us** and the racism and bigotry in our own African American community.

But I'll get to that in just a bit. First it may be best to address the white community and get this part out of the way. Yes, many whites have the racist mentality and some (maybe more than we think) are actually proud of that mentality. But the great thing about dealing with whites who openly display that racist mentality is that we *know* where they're coming from. We know who the enemy is, what he looks like, how he sounds and how he thinks. There's transparency there...and that's the beauty of that scenario.

Don't you want to know who your enemy is so you can learn his habits and how to defeat him? I know I do. That's why I don't harbor any ill will toward white people who openly display their hatred, ill will or so-called superiority toward Blacks. I can deal with the ones who are open about their dislike because there are no surprises there. By being open, they have effectively prepared me for what is coming or what may come in the future. It is those who mask their hatred, racism or ill will that I'm leery of. They are the ones who "seem" to accept Black people but in reality they put every plan they can think of in motion to hold Black people back.

True Story: I grew up with a bunch of country white people. In fact, one of my best friends was white—and country. But he and his family were good people. They knew about racism but they weren't racist. He (my best friend) was white but he didn't have any white friends. His mom was married to a white guy but their family was always surrounded by Black people. I liked their family and they liked me. I ate dinner at their house, went to school with their children, and even listened to country music with them. They never spoke a derogatory word to or about me. It was only after I left this white-washed environment that I understand what racism was.

When I became a teenager, things changed. My friend and his family didn't change, but things changed just the same. There were outside forces at work, I guess you could say. For example, one day my friend and I were walking to the arcade to play video games when someone called me a nigger. It was the first time anyone had ever that tone—that racial bite--to call me that name. I could feel the sarcasm and hatred. I was 14 years old.

One thing I know is this: people aren't born racist. Racism is learned; it's taught. People say we can't live in a race-free society, but I did; I lived in one without knowing what racism was until that day I was called a nigger at age 14.

Back then it was hard to figure racism out; hard to figure out how people really felt about things. But that's not how it is today. Today you can see clearly who likes you and who doesn't. People's true colors are coming out, and the amazing thing is that they don't care. Most people don't even bother to hide how they really feel anymore. In fact, I admit that I myself am a very prejudiced person. We all are, in one way or another. That's why when we set about to figure out who is racist and who is not, we must first look at ourselves and admit that we have all contributed to the current racial climate.

Are You a Racist?

Now that we have white people out of the way it's time to look at ourselves. It's time to call for transparency in our own community because when you have transparency you can see the truth and decide how you're going to deal with it. When you have transparency you realize—however reluctantly—that African Americans are every bit as racist as the people we call racists. That's right, we are as racist as the very people we have problems with.

I'll go a step further: If Blacks were not so racist within our own culture, we might be doing a lot better than we are right now. But we don't want to talk about our own racism. We don't want to talk about how hateful we are to our own people. We don't want to talk about how we hate light-skinned people with long hair, or dark-skinned people with short hair, or people who don't pronounce their words the way we do, or people who have better jobs than we do, or people who go to better (or worse) schools than we do, or people with big noses, or people with lots of money, or people who live in housing projects...or a thousand other variations.

Consider this excerpt from the lyrics of the old 1968 single by Sly and the Family Stone, called *"Everyday People:"*

> *There is a yellow one*
> *That won't accept the black one*
> *That won't accept the red one*
> *That won't accept the white one*
> *Different strokes*
> *For different folks*[55]

According to Wikipedia "this song is one of Sly Stone's pleas for peace and equality between differing races and social groups." It was written nearly 50 years ago and the words are as relevant today as they were when the song debuted. But African Americans don't want to talk about our own prejudices; how our women are envious and suspicious of each other or how our men shoot and kill each other or how none of us—educated, uneducated, rich, poor or middle class—are willing to support our own Black businesses.

We don't want to talk about how our own Black bank cashiers or grocery cashiers can smile and laugh and joke with any other customer, but when a Black person steps up to their counter, the smile

---

[55] Stone, Sly. *Everyday People.* November, 1968.

is quickly replaced by a sneer and a snarky attitude. Some of these cashiers or public servants cannot even bring themselves to say "Hello, how are you today?" to a fellow African American.

There's so much we don't want to talk about. We want transparency but we don't want it when it shines the light on us. We don't want it in our own community. If we had more—or even some—transparency in our communities, we could admit that we are slowly (or rapidly; depends on how you look at it) becoming a community of fat, lazy, uneducated bigots. This is true of every race, yes, but it's especially true of the African American community.

We must focus on a solution, and whatever that solution may be, transparency should be integrated into it. With transparency we can see, define, acknowledge and tackle our issues; we can accept accountability for our faults and shortcomings. This is important because up to now, the African American community has put a lot of thought and energy into blaming others for what is happening with us, but we have left **us** out of the equation.

This blame game has to end sometime, so why not now? Why not engage in self-reflection and accountability as to how we got to where we are today, and how to parachute away from it to a more positive place? We must stop blaming others for what we are and we must stop blaming the white man for something that happened one hundred years ago.

Am I saying that white people aren't part of the problem? No! Should they take accountability for their part in the problem? Yes. Should they—and everyone else, show some emotional understanding about the plight of the African American community? Definitely. All this being said, should we (African Americans) say that people today are responsible for what has happened to us? No, I'm afraid not. They may be contributing to today's climate, but they're definitely not solely responsible for it.

We must focus on a blame-free solution to the problems within the African American community. All of us will be in a better situation when we do because there will at last be some accountability. It's not logical to think that everything is the white man's fault, and until we erase that thinking, we won't be able to move forward.

CHAPTER 8

Accountability

I have mentioned "accountability" over and over in this book, but what exactly does the word mean? Accountability means to be responsible or accept responsibility for something. Except for very young children, everyone should understand this definition; therefore, I'm going to jump right into the discussion and not waste time with a lot of examples. You should know that this chapter is written to put the hard questions to our African American communities, and one of those questions is: what are you going to do about what you've read in this book so far?

The first step in accepting accountability and working within it is to ask yourself this question: How can I be less prejudiced? I gave you examples of our many, many prejudices toward each other in the previous chapter, including prejudice against skin color, body type, hair length, possessions, and bank account(s), to name a few. A few days ago, I read a Facebook post in which someone pointed out that President Obama has suffered more racism, hatred, envy and disrespect than any other president in history. As people across Facebook chimed into the discussion, Black people began to war amongst themselves. Some called President Obama a nigger. Others called the Black people who posted positive things about him "ignorant," "sheeple" and "house niggers." Some wrote the abbreviation "smh" (shaking my head) and went on to say that the only thing Black people do is insult each other and fight among themselves.

As the discussion wore on, each new comment was worse than the last until young Blacks were calling old Blacks "has been's" and "useless." Older Blacks were demanding respect from younger Blacks and insisting that the younger generation has been lost forever, and no one was respecting anyone. I finally navigated away from that sideshow. It was a mess.

My question again is: how can I (and you) be less prejudiced? How can we begin to have intelligent conversations with each other without name-calling, grandstanding and otherwise putting on a circus for the casual bystander—which is usually white people? After all the cursing, complaining, yelling and finger-pointing, what will someone—*anyone*--do next to get the people in our communities back on the right track?

Right about now you may be yelling out, "We have Black Lives Matter!" You're right, we do. But the Black Lives Matter movement isn't offering any solutions for our communities. If Black lives really do matter so much, why are Black people still killing Black people? Why are Black fathers still walking away from their Black wives/girlfriends and Black children and leaving them with no support?

Why are Black people still refusing to support Black businesses? Why are Black parents still neglecting to educate their children instead of doing all they can to keep them out of prison? Why are Black women still starring on derogatory reality shows (aka, "fight clubs" and "diva shows") and giving every other Black woman in the world a bad name? Why are some Black women still leaving their children alone to fend for themselves while they go out and party?

I'll say it again, Black lives don't matter to anyone—especially Black people. And until they do matter to Black people they are definitely not going to matter to anyone else.

Here's a prime example of accountability: Let's say you weigh 375 pounds...which means you're just plain fat. When you go places, people look at you and see a big, fat, overweight person. Some of them may point, some may laugh, some may whisper, and some may just give you the side-eye. Naturally, you don't want them pointing and laughing at you, and you definitely don't want them to think of you as fat. You want them to see you as slim, fit, and attractive. You want them to see you as "thick." But the truth is, you're not thick. You're fat, and that's all there is to it.

Those people see what they see. They see what's right there in front of their eyes. They can't miss it; after all, there's 375 pounds of it staring them in the face. If you practice self-transparency then you'll be truthful with yourself. You will know that you can't truly be angry about what they see. You are the one who has given them a 375-pound body to look at.

If you want people to see you differently, you're going to have to lose some of that fat.

Solutions

We need real solutions. It is possible that the Black Lives Matter campaign was created to give Black people a way to vent their frustrations, but as we all know, venting doesn't change anything. It doesn't offer solutions.

What are Black people doing other than complaining and being mad, to fix the issues in their communities? Unfortunately, the only goal it seems that Black people have achieved is the goal of indecisiveness and playing the blame game. We are the descendants of kings, but at this point we are only the kings of unaccountability.

Let's not continue to be great at complaining while never offering solutions. Remember, we used to have solutions and they worked! Black Wall Street worked. MLK's marches and speeches worked. Malcolm X was a solution that worked. True, all these are gone, but we can compile some new solutions. We can take accountability, restructure our communities, and focus on appropriate relationships, proper education and the protection of our communities. Once we start the process of finding and implementing solutions, there should be no other way to go except up.

CHAPTER 9

Journey to Greatness

Lao Tzu, philosopher and poet of ancient China, once said: "The journey of a thousand miles begins with one step." That is very true. And it is also true that the traveler who is about to make the journey must know his starting point and where he exactly wants to end up so he can map and control his journey.

When it comes to African American history, many people—African Americans included—assume that our journey began with enslavement in America. That couldn't be further from the truth. Our journey began much, much earlier than that. There is a screenshot floating around the Internet that states:

> *"They didn't steal slaves; they stole scientists, doctors, architects, astronomers, teachers, entrepreneurs, fathers, mothers, sons, daughters, etc. and made them slaves."*

I'm not sure who to credit for this profound statement, but I'm in total agreement. African Americans' lives did not begin when we landed on Plymouth Rock (or rather, when it landed on us, as Malcolm X once pointed out), but long before our arrival to America.

In the Introduction to this book I regaled you with a few of our most notable African American ancestors and I told you that we do, indeed, come from royalty. But for the purpose of this chapter, I want to go back even further than this. Back to that early time when man was simply a hunter. When man's sole purpose was to be a hunter and protector within his household and his community.

That purpose hasn't changed, even if the African American community has. The African American male must be a hunter—a leader, an innovator, a provider and a protector. And to become those things, the African American male must be taught by an African American male. Yes I understand that it is women that perform the bulk of nurturing when it comes to caring for sons and daughters, often because there is no adult male around and they have no choice. A woman can be a protector, a nurturer, a confidante and a friend to her sons...but she can't teach a prince to be a king. She can't help a man be a man. Another man—typically the father—must fill this role.

It is my belief and experience that by adolescence (age twelve), it is important for a man-child to understand the foundation of being a man. Of course, there is no real reason for a child to "become a man" at such an early age anymore because we do not live in an environment where we must hunt for food all the day long. (Actually, this last statement is arguable, but for purposes of this chapter, we're going to assume it's true). Since we no longer need our twelve-year-old boys to be hunters, we look to the next best parallel role. In this case, we would say that a man needs to learn how to get a job and secure it so that he can prepare to take his place in society.

Learning how to find, get and keep a job is equivalent to a man learning to "perfect his process of becoming a man/hunter/protector."

Only when the man perfects this process should he bring his queen into his kingdom, and they two should build an empire and a family.

Every culture has a time to take this "man journey;" to gain leadership and creativity skills that will help a man-child perfect his process so he can become the best man/hunter/protector there is. For example, the Jewish community has the Bar Mitzvah where thirteen-year-old boys (and girls) demonstrate their commitment to their faith and also show that they recognize they are responsible for following Jewish law. The Amish celebrate Rumspringa, during which time sixteen-year-old youth get to enjoy their first unsupervised weekends away from family and "enjoy whatever pleasure they like, be it alcohol or clothing."[56] This way they get to see and experience the world, see if they are missing anything, and return of their own choice as committed community members.

Inuit boys go out into the wilderness with their fathers at the tender age of eleven and twelve. There they test their hunting skills and learn how to acclimate themselves to bitterly cold weather. And among the Maasai of Kenya and Tanzania "boys between the ages of 10-20 are initiated into a warrior class." Among other activities, the boys "sleep outside in the forest...drink a mixture of alcohol, cow's blood, and milk, while also consuming large portions of meat...and are later circumcised, making the official transformation into a man, warrior, and protector. [The] boys cannot flinch because doing so would shame their families and discount their bravery.[57]

In America, sixteen-year-olds are considered legally permitted to drive a car (after they pass the required tests, of course). Getting that first permit is like a rite of passage, and is usually followed by a

---

[56] Pfeffer, Leticia. "13 Amazing Coming of Age Traditions From Around the World." GlobalCitizen.org. https://www.globalcitizen.org/en/content/13-amazing-coming-of-age-traditions-from-around-th/. Retrieved February 3, 2016.
[57] Ibid.

sweet sixteen party that is a type of "coming of age" or "coming out into society" party. African Americans, however, do not have a specific ritual to mark their transition from childhood to manhood. They also do not have a specific time when this transition is set into motion. Why? Because African Americans live in a largely matriarchal society, and again, a woman cannot help a man become a man.

Not making this transition can be devastating for a young man. Why? Because according to an article called *Boys' Rite of Passage: Boy to Man Transition*, "without some form of official closure to childhood and welcoming to manhood, a male can become caught in a subconscious life long quest to have that affirmation that he is indeed a man."[58] The article goes on to say that boys who have not made this transition try to confirm their manhood in other unspoken ways, like:

- Being a workaholic.
- Alcohol consumption.
- Sports involvement.
- Sexual conquests.
- Heroic exploits (bungee jumping etc.).
- Marriage.
- Promotions at work.[59]

In the African American community, not having a specific rite of passage at a specific time simply leaves our young men "hanging out there." They may assume any of the characteristics in the above bullet points. They may also join gangs because that is what they think being a man is, or they may degrade women because that is what they think a man does. They may be overly aggressive toward one another,

---

[58] "Used by permission Copyright 1998-2016 http://boysunderattack.com" All rights reserved. http://boysunderattack.com/man.html. Retrieved on February 3, 2016.
[59] Ibid.

threaten one another, develop a hair-trigger temper, or any number of characteristics that they *think* proves that they are men.

In the journey from where we are to where we want to be, we must consider how we will guide and transition our sons into the men they need to be for all of the African American queens out there who are waiting to be found.

CHAPTER 10

Come, Black Queen

N ow that we know where our journey begins—which is at the feet of the young African American male who must transition his way from prince to king, it is time to discuss the type of African American queen who should be waiting for him at the culmination of his transition.

A queen is historically displayed as someone who is born into royalty. If she is not a direct product of someone already sitting on the throne, she is daughter of a royal son, daughter or cousin who is "in line" to ascend to the throne. She is usually raised in affluence and bred in culture and etiquette. She knows who she is and what is expected of her. If she is not trained to rule directly, she is trained to stand beside the ruler (as wife or confidante) and offer dignity, loyalty, comfort, support and beauty.

A queen is typically someone that other women aspire to look like, act like, talk like and dress like. Knowing the immense and far-reaching influence she can have, she usually displays impeccable taste, unquestionable manners, and admirable generosity in philanthropy and social causes. She is expected to be conservative in dress, but she is also expected to exude understated elegance. She is expected to be modest and yet dashingly beautiful. In addition, her morals, scruples and personal reputation are all expected to be unquestioned. These are big shoes to fill indeed, but we are talking about a woman who would be queen, after all.

Where does the African American woman fit in this royal scheme of things? Can she fill these royal shoes?

Background of Female Coming-of-Age Rituals

We have already discussed how other races help their sons to transition from childhood to adulthood and we have shown how, unfortunately, African Americans largely fail to perform this ritual with our sons so that they know how to take their place in society. Now it is time to examine our daughters and see what we're working with; see how our portrayal in the media has influenced how they see themselves.

Two of the better-known practices that African Americans engage in to help our daughters enter into society as proper young women are cotillions and Sweet 16 parties. Without naming specific organizations, we can say that there are many sororities that host cotillion or debutante balls where young girls are "presented to society under the lights of elegance and the approval of their family and friends."[60] These girls are introduced to the family's social and business network, and to society as a whole. They learn etiquette, good behavior, and also how to dress well. But the main purpose of the cotillion is to help these girls find suitable husbands.

Although cotillions and debutante balls are wonderful and worthy practices, they were initially "a way for wealthy and middle-

---

[60] Fields, Dorothy Jenkins, PhD. Black in Time: The Tradition of Cotillion and Beautillion Balls Continues. May 28, 2015. MiamiHerald.com. http://www.miamiherald.com/news/local/community/miami-dade/community-voices/article22549722.html. Retrieved on February 4, 2014.

class Blacks to demonstrate their achievements,"[61] evidenced by the fact that many of these girls went on to marry well, or to study law or medicine. And although cotillions have changed somewhat since their initial debut so that they are now more inclusive, many poorer Blacks feel that Blacks who participate in such rituals "want to be viewed as separate and *above* Blacks in the hood. They long to be looked up to, to be admired and revered and to wield authority no matter how slight or insignificant."[62] Believing this, many Blacks did not (and still don't) even attempt to participate in such rituals, which means that their daughters did not (and still don't) participate either.

In addition to Black cotillions, most if not all of America has heard of the "Sweet 16 Party." The Sweet 16 is a coming-of-age party that celebrates several milestones. First, it marks the passage from girlhood to young womanhood. Second, it means that the girl has reached the legal age to obtain a driver's permit to begin driving. And third, it marks the age at which the girl can get her first job and begin learning how to handle money, hone her skills and talents, and get along with diverse personalities.

Some of the rituals within the Sweet 16 ritual include:

- **Dancing with her father,** during which time all eyes are on her and she feels special, and not like just one of the crowd. By dancing with her, the father demonstrates his love for her and pride in her, and he treats her like "the princess that she is." This dance also shows her how a real man would and should treat a woman he loves.

- **Getting a family heirloom as a keepsake**, which symbolizes the older generation expressing its love, support

---

[61] Hahn, Christopher. The Lost History of Black Cotillions. Drew.edu. Drew University. http://www.drew.edu/news/2010/11/15/thelosthistoryofblackcotillions. Retrieved on February 4, 2016.

[62] Milton. "Black Hypocrisy: Black Elite, Church Folk and Obama." BlackQuillAndInk.com. Retrieved from http://blackquillandink.com/?p=17867 on February 4, 2016.

and admiration for the younger generation; and the older generation's hope and belief that the younger generation will keep the family tradition alive.

- **Receiving high-heeled shoes.** Although this part of the tradition is not as widely known as the other parts, it is equally as symbolic. The girl wears flat shoes to her party, and at some point her father, uncle or a male relative ceremoniously brings her a pair of high heel shoes to wear, sometimes laid out on a satin pillow. This symbolizes the world's recognition of her formal transition to young womanhood.

- **Receiving a tiara.** This is usually presented by the mother and symbolizes that the daughter has become a woman. It may also be a way of saying, "Always remember that you are a princess."

There are, of course, many other coming-of-age rituals out there. However, since we are focusing our attention on young African American women, we feel that the above will suffice.

What We Have

The above coming-of-age rituals are not only beautiful, they are important because they help the young girl recognize who she is, where she's going, what is expected of her, and what she should expect in return. But what happens if the girl's parents do not get her involved in these rituals? In fact, what happens if they leave her to her own devices to figure out what a woman is, what she has to offer, and what she should be looking for in a man?

These questions may represent what is already happening in the African American community. Every other race makes it a point to teach their daughters manners, etiquette, good grooming, good men, and what to strive for in life. Every other race tells their daughters what a woman is and what is expected of her. And every other race tells their daughters how to keep themselves; that there's nothing wrong with not sleeping around or being the most popular and sought after girl in the community.

Unfortunately, this often doesn't happen in the African American community. More often than not, our young African American girls waste their youth and their beauty on absolute foolishness. African American girls seem to want to be known as 'hoes' and 'bitches.' Many don't think there's anything wrong with being called 'THOTs' (that ho' over there) or sluts. Some are proud to be called 'big-bootie ho's and yearn to be featured in videos where they get to shake their behind and show everyone what they have.

African American girls and women have no problem being loud, brash, profane and threatening, both in public and in private. Some are proud of their hair-trigger tempers and boast about how quickly they will beat another bitch's ass if she disrespects her. Some have no problem leaving their young children unattended while they party it up on the weekends because they feel they deserve it. Just recently, an article appeared on the Internet about a stripper who left her two-year-old daughter alone all night so she could go to work. When she returned home at 9:30am the next morning, her toddler was dead, burned to death in an apartment fire.[63] Yes, this happens in other communities, too, but this book is about the African American community.

Sadly, between the ages of 16 to 35 (and sometimes woefully younger) our girls and young women waste time on the wrong activities, the wrong men, the wrong priorities, the wrong goals, and the wrong results. By the time many of them are 35 years of age they

[63] Parascandola, Roscoe et. al. "Stripper Mom Who Partied as 2-Year Old Daughter Died Alone in Brooklyn House Fire Was Already Under Investigation." New York Daily News. http://www.nydailynews.com/new-york/stripper-mom-tot-fire-death-investigation-article-1.2542325. Retrieved on February 26, 2016.

have already experienced one or two divorces and are left to raise a bunch of children alone.

Our girls give themselves whole-heartedly to the wrong men because they are chasing men who don't even exist. What I mean is, instead of taking the time to get to know the man and find out what he is about and what he is capable of, they dream of taming the 'bad boy' or being showered with money by the rich boy. Never mind that the rich boy may be selling enough drugs to buy an entire country; as long as he is bringing some of that money home to them, they're okay with it.

Other African American girls see with their own eyes how scarce African American men are, and how those that are not killed at a young age or left languishing in jail are flocking to any other race *except* African American women. Therefore, these girls believe that they must hurry and give themselves to any man who shows them a bit of attention before someone else snatches him up. After all, there's a saying out there that "whatever one woman won't do there are ten other women who will." So our girls accept anything that comes their way, and then once they have him, they find themselves miserable and in a world of trouble because of his drug addiction or his drug business or his absenteeism or his laziness or domestic violence, or any number of other negative qualities.

By the time the average African American girl/woman figures out what a good man is as opposed to what she *thought*, a real good man doesn't even want her. I know this is difficult to hear but it's true: by the time these poor, misguided, world-weary young women discover the depth of the garbage surrounding the Black men they have chosen to consort with, their own choices have drastically diminished. As some like to put it, "the pickings are mighty slim."

Ignorance, poor parenting, and low self-esteem are ruining our African American women. With no guide to teach our young girls what a woman is, how to know when she has become a woman, and how to carry herself once she has, our women are like leaves in the wind. They are being blown everywhere.

What We Need

We need more Black queens. To get them, we will have to begin with shaping and fashioning Black princesses. We have already described the qualities of a queen, so now we will describe the queen's characteristics. A queen knows who she is. She knows that she is worth a great price—not because she has a huge behind, big boobs and a small waist, but because of her character and what she brings to the table.

And what is it that she brings to the table? She brings patience, kindness and intelligence. That's right, she is not stupid. She is also not loud, brash, or argumentative. Not to say that she can't express her opinions; only that she expresses them in a reasonable way.

A queen is self-possessed and also shows pride in herself. To that end, she doesn't throw her body at every man whose shadow crosses her path, even if she does believe that there's a shortage of men out there. She doesn't refer to herself as a 'big-bootie ho', nor does she allow her so-called man to speak about her that way. She doesn't giggle when a man calls her a bitch, nor does she shake her ass because some thug wants to see what she can do with it. She doesn't strip because it's quick and easy money; she doesn't 'trick' because her boyfriend tells her she should be willing to do it if she really loves him.

A queen doesn't think of future children as a way to get child support or food stamps or free lunches any other type of aid. She doesn't think of future children as a way to trap a man who she can clearly see is a bum, a drug dealer or a womanizer. She thinks of future children as gifts from God and the jewels of her old age, if she lives that long.

A queen is tender and respectful toward her man, but perhaps her best quality is that she WILL NEVER allow him to run over her. She lets him know in no uncertain terms that she WON'T be working like a man to keep him happy; however, he is more than welcome to work like the man that he is to keep *her* happy. She tells her man that if she does anything for him at all, it's because she wants to do it. It's because it's in her nature to do it, and not because she owes it to him or is trying to prove anything to him.

A true queen knows she has nothing to prove.

The sad truth in today's African American community is that many Black men expect their women to work, pay the bills, buy them clothes, give them spending money, and NOT ask where they are going or when they are coming back. Many times, if a woman refuses to give up her money, or if she doesn't give up enough of it, the Black man will walk out on her without a backward glance. This is why a true queen has been trained early on to choose her man wisely so that she doesn't experience this sort of foolishness. And if she does experience it—because relationships like these happen to everyone at one time or another—she quickly eases her head out of the lion's mouth and gets the hell out of there.

A true queen realizes that she doesn't have to be treated like a mule or a pack horse just to be able to say that she has a boyfriend or a husband. A true queen doesn't necessarily want to be on her on, but she is perfectly fine if that's the way it has to be.

A queen learns how to handle her money early. She knows how to manage her own household, hold down a job, juggle college classes, and set goals for herself. By learning how to be independent and do these things for herself, she is effectively preparing herself for the man who "finds" her, marries her, and begins to build a legacy with her.

Target the King

Since we have already discussed what a king is, we should be able to move smoothly ahead and talk about how to target a king. First of all, the word "king" is a masculine word—which means the *man* is supposed to be the king, not the woman. A woman shouldn't want to be with a man who isn't a leader, provider, and protector in the marriage and in the community. She shouldn't even look his way if he is anything less than these.

Here are some characteristics of a true king:

1. A king already knows he is a man and doesn't feel the need to prove it.

2. A king knows that his seed will be royal, so he does not just settle for any woman; he seeks the right woman to bear his seed and help to build his royal house.

3. A king knows that he is the stronger vessel and his wife is the weaker vessel. Therefore, he always treats her as the weaker vessel, like a delicate flower that should be nourished, protected, and respected.

4. A king has his life together. He is a leader and a provider; he's a man who not only knows how to earn money, but he knows where that money should be spent.

5. A king doesn't try to be "what's cool." He recognizes that what's cool doesn't pay the bills.

6. A king has a financial obligation to take care of his woman and accepts that obligation with the right attitude.

7. A king allows his woman to work but he doesn't force her to work.

8. A king does not leave his woman to do everything by herself; he shares the decision-making, the plans and the child-rearing.

When the queen finds her king, only then can they create an empire and a legacy. I will discuss more about what a legacy is and how you can build one in Chapter 12. In the meantime, just know that the only way to build a legacy is to do so within a loving relationship and controlled environment where the parents know their roles and the children have the best opportunity to learn.

CHAPTER 11

Feeding Royalty

W hat does one feed a queen? It's an important question. If it's true that "you are what you eat," it is up to the African American community to make sure that our members—especially our queens—eat only the best.

But as always, first things first: we must admit that the way our community eats is a BIG problem that produces BIG men and women. As a whole, our community has adopted some absolutely horrible eating habits. Other cultures make it a point to eat healthy. Even the African culture east healthy, but when it comes to selecting and maintaining a balanced diet, African Americans are woefully off course.

While we're on the subject, it should be noted that the whole "BBW" (big, beautiful women) concept and way of life is off kilter. Not to say that "thick" Black women can't be beautiful; only that a fat woman needn't delude herself into thinking that the "I'm-thick-and-beautiful" mantra is going to change the fact that she's just downright fat.

The goal here is not to insist that all Black women must have one body style or type—*thin*. Rather, the goal is healthy eating and nothing more. America is the most obese country in the entire world and according to StateOfObesity.org, African Americans have the highest obesity rates among adults by race and ethnicity: (Black – 47.8%; Latino – 42.5%; White – 32.6%).[64] The conclusion: "Communities of color have been hit especially hard by the obesity epidemic."[65]

So why are African Americans so fat? There are many reasons, which include "disparate access to healthy and affordable food, safe places to be physically active, living in low-income communities that have limited access to supermarkets and fresh produce, and higher exposure to marketing of less nutritious foods.[66] For example, "billboards and other forms of outdoor advertisements which…promote foods of low nutritional value are 13 times denser in predominantly African American neighborhoods than White neighborhoods.[67] Also, "Black high school students are almost twice as likely to not eat breakfast daily compared with their White peers, which can be a contributing factor to less healthy eating patterns overall, weight gain and poorer performance in school."[68]

The above are only examples of some of the problem areas that affect obesity rates in the African American community. They ARE NOT an exhaustive list by any stretch of the imagination. Why is it important to be aware of these rates and numbers? Because they affect our community's health (80% of obese people have Type 2 Diabetes);

---

[64] The State of Obesity: Better Policies For a Healthier America. StateofObesity.org. Retrieved on February 10, 2016 - http://stateofobesity.org/disparities/.

[65] Ibid.

[66] Ibid.

[67] Yancey AK, Cole BL, et al. A cross-sectional prevalence study of ethnically targeted and general audience outdoor-related advertising. *Milbank Q*, 2009: 87(1): 155-184, 2009.

[68] U.S. Centers for Disease Control and Prevention. Youth Risk Behavior Surveillance — United States, 2013. *Morbidity and Mortality Weekly Report*, **63**(SS04): 1-168, 2014

mortality rates (death from heart disease and strokes are twice as high among African Americans as Whites); and they send our medical costs soaring into the stratosphere (medical costs associated with obesity were as high as $190 billion dollars in 2005).

What We Can Do?

We can make it our business to do something about our health. There are already many nutritional programs in existence, but it is up to us to make the best use of these programs. We can take it upon ourselves to learn more about proper nutrition online or via a nutrition program. For example, those who have been diagnosed with diabetes are usually given access to a licensed nutritionist who can help them plan and execute nutritionally sound meals. Also, we can use "SNAP-Ed, the partnership between USDA and the states that provide education to help families learn how to eat healthier within a limited budget."[69]

There are also free resources online.

1. Sparkpeople.com provides free tools, resources and support for adults who want to improve their diets and/or manage their weight.

2. Nutrition.gov is a gateway to reliable information on nutrition, healthy eating, physical activity, and food safety for consumers.

3. USDA.gov lists a bevy of websites that can help both you and your child to lose weight and improve your eating habits.

---

[69] Food Research and Action Center. A Review of Strategies to Bolster SNAP's Role in Improving Nutrition as well as Food Security. Washington, D.C.: FRAC, 2013. (accessed May 2014).

This is by no means an exhaustive list. Use your favorite search engine to find many more resources that cost you absolutely nothing to try out.

CHAPTER 12

Building a Legacy

After all is said and done and after we have identified our challenges, addressed them, attempted to fix them, and even attempted to educate our community on the benefits of health and fitness, it is time. Time for us to build a legacy.

What is a legacy? It is something of value that is transmitted by or received from an ancestor or predecessor. In the case of this book, a legacy is not something that those of us who are reading this book are waiting to receive; it is something of value that those of us who are reading this book want to leave to our loved ones so that each generation after us will be better than our own generation.

For purposes of this book, we are going to break the concept of "legacy" into two parts: Marriage and Courting. Why? Because the end result should be marriage, family and legacy building. And we definitely want to make sure that our community builds its families the correct way.

Courting and Marriage

There are many types of families in the world, and in the African American community. There are two-parent families, single-parent families, and families where grandparents must raise the children because the parents are MIA (missing-in-action). However, it is our strong belief that the only way to build a solid and effective legacy is to start with a strong, traditional family. How do we do this? We begin with "courting."

To court means "be involved with romantically; to pay special attention to someone in an attempt to win their support or favor, typically with the intention of marrying." Notice that the last part stated *typically with the intention of marrying.* It did not specify that courting should be done with the intention of sleeping with someone a hundred times to see if you're a match; or with the intention of adding another woman to your stable or another man to your collection. It should not be done with the intention of "shacking up" or experimenting to see how much money you can get out of a man or how many women you can have in every city—or neighborhood, for that matter. And it should not be done because you're "finding yourself" or "sowing your wild oats." You court someone with the intention of marrying them.

To begin courting, you should recognize and welcome the fact that your parents should have a say-so. After all, your parents know you; they know your ways, your quirks, your idiosyncrasies, and your aspirations. Your parents have been around the block and know all the tricks a young man or woman might tend to play with you—tricks you probably won't be able to identify because you're too in love to notice.

Parents can typically see through all the b*llshit. Parents aren't looking at your beloved with rose-colored glasses; they look at your beloved with all the scrutiny a car buyer uses when he's considering buying a car. Your parents will kick the proverbial tires, check the proverbial odometer to see how many miles is on this particular car, and check under the hood to make sure the engine hasn't been souped up to enhance performance.

These and many other reasons are why parents in the African American community should become actively involved in the person their son or daughter intends to court. The truth is that African Americans allow their children to date too early. Many feel that "testing the waters" is not a bad thing for males—or even females. Unfortunately, testing the waters often leads to teen pregnancies, abortions, abandonment, baby-mama-drama, and/or single-parent homes.

In order to build a legacy, the home's foundation must be solid and strong. The two people who are forming the legacy must love and respect each other, because if they do not, it will be only too easy to leave their other half swinging alone in the breeze. Here are a few steps of courtship:

Meet the Parents

Your son or daughter's new beau should have to come to your home to meet you BEFORE he or she is allowed to go out on the town with your child. This public acknowledgement of interest helps the couple to feel a certain level of commitment toward the courtship, and to treat it with a degree of dignity and respect.

Courting vs. Dating

It's important that you (and by default, your children) know the difference between dating and courtship. Dating usually begins when two people meet and want to get to know each other. They may talk on the telephone, go to the movies or go out for a bite to eat. They feel no obligation to each other at that time. However long their time together may be, they just engage in activities together to see if they *like the* other person enough to become a couple. This "spending time" may also include kissing, exchanging flowers and letters, heavy petting or even sex. But no matter how much or little is involved in these activities, the couple usually enters into this arrangement with the understanding that absolutely nothing may come of it. They may even know that the other person is dating someone else at the same time they are dating them.

Courtship is the same...but different. The couple may talk on the telephone and go to the movies or out to eat. They may exchange flowers and letters and spend time together with or without the other's family, but this is as far as the similarities go. The courting couple does not just court mindlessly, like the dating couple. The courting couple expects something out of the courtship, and that something is eventual marriage.

Also, the courting couple DOES NOT engage in sex during the courtship period. They may not engage in heavy petting, not because they are so perfect or so religious, but because they understand that this may fuel the desire for sex when that desire is not their end-goal. Their true desire is for marriage. Therefore, these activities are reserved for when they have made their lasting and permanent commitment to each other. Instead of tempting each other beyond endurance, they spend this time and energy with the goal of getting engaged or married and determining whether the person they are courting is "the one."

90-Days to Know You

It doesn't take forever to figure out whether you really want to be with a person. Young couples should agree on spending a certain amount of time together to decide whether they are compatible and can move to the next step in the game of love. That amount of time can be 90 days or even as much as 6 months or a year. Whatever the couple agrees on, they should also acknowledge that while they are getting to know each other they will refrain from courting/dating anyone else. Obviously not every courtship will end in marriage, but the partners should at least feel free enough to let their feelings unfold without worrying that the other person is considering other partners.

Declaring Intentions

During the "getting to know you" phase, couples should declare their intentions to each other. They should discuss what it is each of them wants, and they should listen to what the other person wants. This is vital, because today's Black woman has no clue what a Black man wants, and today's Black man has no clue what the woman wants. In other words, everybody's in the dark.

If the woman wants to wait before having children (after the couple is married), now is the time to tell the man. If he wants her to be a stay-at-home wife, he had better tell her before they say "I do." This exchange of intentions will move the couple one step closer to deciding whether they are compatible in one or more areas, or whether their ideas are so different that they cannot possibly remain together.

No Ring, No Sex!

African American parents should teach their daughters NOT to have sex with their boyfriends until a commitment has been made. Many parents say they teach this, but if they do, it certainly doesn't show. In fact, many parents have given up trying to teach this concept and simply put their daughters on birth control pills at as young an age as possible. But in the case of courtship, abstinence is imperative. If the couple becomes sexually active before committing to each other, the odds of ending up with an unwanted pregnancy are pretty high. And if that happens, the couple will have perpetuated what is already going on in the African American community: rampant sexual activity and a huge number of illegitimate babies that are typically dumped on the single mother for care.

All this being said, parents should teach their sons that "if you don't want to put a ring on her finger, you get no sex. Period."

Marriages

After a proper courtship, the couple can move on toward marriage. However, they do not necessarily need to rush into it. It is expected that both parties prepare themselves for marriage. The young man should be well-versed on what it means to be a man, what it takes to assume responsibility for a wife, what it takes to get a good job, what it takes to hold onto it, what it entails to bring a family into the world, and how to build substance while building a legacy.

The young woman should understand what it takes to please a man, why it is important to allow a man to lead, what it means to be a mother, why it may be necessary to work outside the home to help her husband bring money into the home, and how to play her part in building a legacy.

Conclusion

N ow that we know all these things, where do we go from here? It's up to us, really. The African American community is unique in every way. We have history and culture, and yet we are much like a new race or species: we don't have our own language and we certainly don't have our own ancestral history. In fact, we are the only race that has been totally stripped of our language, our culture, our history, and even our dietary habits.

Think about it, every other race has been allowed to maintain their culture. When you make telephone calls to large and small companies today, the first thing you are instructed to do is "Press 1 for Spanish." ATM's also have other language options but...have you ever received any instruction to "Press 1 for Swahili?" or "Press 1 for Somali?" or "Arabic?" No, you have not. That is because no one seems interested in the African language.

One other question: Is our food really our food, or does it belong to some other culture? For example, African Americans are supposedly "known" for foods like chittlin's, neck bones, barbecue, pig feet, and an assortment of vegetables and other soul food,[70] but these

---

[70] Soul Food: A Brief History. African American Registry. http://www.aaregistry.org/historic_events/view/soul-food-brief-history. Retrieved February

foods originated during slavery when African Americans were given left-over's to eat. So this means that African Americans aren't really known for these foods at all.

African Americans are all alone on this planet. We don't identify with Whites, Native Americans, Asians, Africans, or even other Black people. We are unique; we are not gay, we are not white, we are not Spanish, and we are not African.

African Americans have no idea what their true identity is. Everyone loves everything African Americans do, but they do not love us. They love our hairstyles, our tan skin color, our vernacular, our handshakes, our dances, our clothing, our jokes and our women. Everyone loves to say "Some of my best friends are Black," but they do not want to be African American because they know that if they became African American they would be all alone on the planet.

Where do we go from here? It is up to us. But one thing is certain; we won't get where we're going until we move from where we are and start walking. That's where this book comes in; it marks our starting place. The rest – the walk to victory – is up to us.

10, 2016.

Bibliography

African American Registry. "Soul Food: A Brief History."
    http://www.aaregistry.org/historic_events/view/soul-food-
    brief-history.

Alcindor, Yamiche. "Civil Rights Leaders at Odds as Ferguson Protests
    Grow." USA Today. USAToday.com.
    http://www.usatoday.com/story/news/nation/2014/12/28/as
    -ferguson-protest-grows-so-do-tensions/20664395/.

AtlantaBlackStar.com staff. "African Kings and Queens Whose Stories
    Must Be Told on Film."
http://atlantablackstar.com/2013/12/07/10-african-kings-and-
    queens-whose-stories-must-be-told-on-film/.

Ax, Joseph. "NY Policeman Guilty of Manslaughter in Shooting of Un
    armed Black Man." Reuters. February 12, 2016.
    http://www.reuters.com/article/us-new-york-police-
    idUSKCN0VL01X.

Bay View. "What Happened to Black Wall Street on June 1, 1921?"
    Sfbayview.com. February 9, 2011.
    http://sfbayview.com/2011/02/what-happened-to-black-
    wall-street-on-june-1-1921/.

Boys Under Attack. "Used by permission Copyright 1998-2016
    http://boysunderattack.com" All rights reserved.
    http://boysunderattack.com/man.html.

Byng, Rhonesha. "The Images of Black Women in the Media 'Still Only
    Scratch the Surface', EssenceStudy Finds."
    HuffingtonPost.com. http://www.huffingtonpost.com/
    2013/10/15/ the-images-of-black-women-in-   me
    dia_n_4102322.html.

Cos Cause. From "We Can't Blame White People."
Snopes.com.http://www.snopes.com/politics/soapbox/cosby.
asp

Davis, Viola [on being a dark-skin black woman in Hollywood]: "The
paper bag test is still alive." TheGrio.com. June 26, 2015.
http://thegrio.com/2015/06/26/viola-davis-hollywood- ste
reotypes-paper-bag-test/.

Fields, Dorothy Jenkins, PhD. "Black in Time: The Tradition of
Cotillion and Beautillion Balls Continues." May 28, 2015.
MiamiHerald.com.
http://www.miamiherald.com/news/local/community/miami
-dade/community-voices/article22549722.html.

Food Research and Action Center. "A Review of Strategies to Bolster
SNAP's Role in Improving Nutrition as well as Food Security."
Washington, D.C.: FRAC, 2013.

Hahn, Christopher. "The Lost History of Black Cotillions."
Drew.edu. Drew University.
http://www.drew.edu/news/2010/11/15/thelosthistoryof
blackcotillions.

Imhotep, Dr. David. The First Americans were Africans:
Documented Evidence.

Kalahar, Dean. "The Decline of the African American Family."
AmericanThinker.com, http://www.americanthinker.
com/artcles/2014/03/the_decline_of_the_africanamerican_
family.html.

Massey, Douglas. Categorically Unequal: The American Stratification System. Russell Sage Foundation, New York, 2007.

Mathis, Judge Greg. The Judge Mathis Show. "Ashamed of Her Race." Season Ten: 2008-2009. 11/12/2008

Milton. "Black Hypocrisy: Black Elite, Church Folk and Obama." BlackQuillAndInk.com. http://blackquillandink.com/?p=17867

Mullins, Dexter. "Survivors of Infamous 1921 Tulsa Race Riot Still Hope for Justice." Aljazeera America. Aljazeera.com. http://america.aljazeera.com/articles/2014/7/19/survivors-of-infamous1921tulsaraceriotstillhopeforjustice.html.

New African Magazine. "How the US Government Used Black People as Guinea Pigs." NewAfricanMagazine.com. http://newafricanmagazine.com/medical-scandal/.

Nittle, Nadra Kareem. "What is Internal Racism?" About News. About.com. http://racerelations.about.com /od/understandingrac1/a/internalizedracism.htm.

Orfield, Gary and Chungmei Lee, "Historic Reversals, Accelerating Resegregation, and the Need for New Integration Strategies," Civil Rights Project, UCLA, August 2007.

Pager, Devah. "The Mark of a Criminal Record," American Journal of Sociology, Volume 108, Number 5, March 2003, pp. 937-75.

Parascandola, Roscoe et. al. "Stripper Mom Who Partied as 2-Year Old Daughter Died Alone in Brooklyn House Fire Was Already Under Investigation." New York Daily News.

http://www.nydailynews.com/new-york/stripper-mom-tot-fire-death-investigation-article-1.2542325.

Pfeffer, Leticia. "13 Amazing Coming of Age Traditions From Around the World." GlobalCitizen.org. https://www.globalcitizen.org/en/content/13-amazing- coming-of-age-traditions-from-around-th/.

Pickens, Josie. "The Destruction of Black Wall Street." Ebony.com. May 31, 2013. http://www.ebony.com/black-history/the-destruction-of-black-wall-street-405#axzz3wyW42HIL.

Quigley, Bill. "Fourteen Examples of Racism in Criminal Justice System." HuffingtonPost.com. http://www.huffingtonpost.com/bill-quigley/fourteen- examples-of-raci_b_658947.html.

Rashidi, Rumoko. Before Enslavement: Africa's Ancient Diaspora. *Atlanta Black Star*. AtlantaBlackStar.com. http://atlantablackstar.com/2014/09/14/enslavment-africas-ancient-diaspora/

Smiley, Tavis, editor. The Covenant with Black America. Third World Press, Chicago, 2006, as cited from David Satcher's essay at the book's website covenantwithblackamerica.com.

Snowden, Ashley. Before We Were Slaves: Great Kings and Queens of Africa. https://thesummary.wordpress.com /2011/08/28/before-we-were-slaves-great-kings-and-queens-of-africa/.

StateofObesity.org. "The State of Obesity: Better Policies For a Healthier America." http://stateofobesity.org/disparities/.

Stone, Sly. Everyday People. November, 1968.

U.S. Centers for Disease Control and Prevention. Youth Risk Behavior Surveillance — United States, 2013. Morbidity and Mortality Weekly Report, 63(SS04): 1-168, 2014

Watkins, Lawrence M. "4 half-truths about black-owned businesses — and why you should still buy blac." The Grio. TheGrio.com. http://thegrio.com/2012/07/23/4-half-truths-about-black-owned-businesses-and-why-you-should-still-buy-black/.

Wikipedia, Free Dictionary. https://en.wikipedia.org/wiki/Omarosa.

Wilkinson, James. "Nearly 15k People Protest in New York over Asian-American Cop's Manslaughter Conviction For Shooting Un armed Black Man." DailyMail.com. February 21, 2016. http://www.dailymail.co.uk/news/article-3456387/Thousands-rally-NYC-US-officers-conviction.html.

Yancey AK, Cole BL, et al. "A cross-sectional prevalence study of eth nically targeted and general audience outdoor-related adver tising." Milbank Q, 2009: 87(1): 155-184, 2009.

Young, Iris. Five Faces of Oppression. "Oppression, Privilege and Resistance." McGraw Hill, Boston. 2004.

ABOUT THE AUTHOR

Race Cummings is the CEO of LinkMeRight Marketing, which specializes in increasing online visibility and promoting the brands of innovative and ambitious professionals; and RaceDreamer Marketing, which specializes in increasing the online presence of and re-branding of small businesses. He is the author of *America: A Race of Victims*; and *Winning the Game: How to Become a Game Changer*. Mr. Cummings resides in Atlanta, Georgia. He welcomes your feedback, and can be reached at RaceCummings@LinkMeRight.net